International Student Handbook

Cover design and image illustrations by Mariana Stacey:
https://www.instagram.com/magsiux/
Copy editing by Sam Wright
eBook and Paperback formatting by Michael Frank

Library of Congress Control Number: 2020913534

ISBN (paperback): 978-1-7354516-0-2
ISBN (ebook): 978-1-7354516-2-6
www.internationalstudenthandbook.com

Introduction

For many students, it's a dream to leave their hometown to study somewhere else. They've only heard from others on what they can expect from their social and academic lives. For some, their career is top of mind and a focus from the beginning of their journey. Whatever your reason for wanting to leave, talking to someone or reading something doesn't compare to the experience of living through it. It gets real, fast. My personal example of when it hit me in the head I was no longer living at home, that I was out there all alone, was when I discovered dryer lint. In the U.A.E., where I grew up, we dried our clothes outdoors on a clothesline. We had a dryer but rarely used it, and I wasn't aware that dryer machines had a part that collected lint, and that it had to be removed after every cycle. I remember calling my mom and telling her "the machines here in the U.S. are different, you have to take out the lint when your clothes finish drying". She laughed at me. I'm sure secretly she also prayed that I could survive the rest of the year.

I was a kid. No REAL life experiences. I had to learn such basic things about taking care of my apartment and my stuff. Then there is managing your time, getting to class, making food, etc. Then there is a small thing called culture shock, and you being where you don't have your familiar home to go back to at the end of the night, forcing you to adapt quickly. And so on . . .

With all that going on, you have to figure out how to keep your grades up, and then at one point (sooner than you think), how to start your career. It's daunting to think about your career at such a time when dealing with all these changes. That's the extra challenge that international students have. But that is also where your energy will develop, why you will come out of this different and stronger than others who didn't leave home to continue their university education. With your original culture, and your experience adapting to a new one, you will come out with an advantage when you are done.

This advantage matters to companies. They just can't easily see it. You have to show it to them.

In this book, I offer my perspective from years of experience studying and working in the U.S. to help show you what to expect from this journey, how to manage yourself, and how to get a head start with your career. I'll show you the picture of the puzzle, I'll tell you about the pieces that matter, but ultimately, it's up to you to put it all together in life.

*"**Believe you can** and you're halfway there."*

~ Theodore Roosevelt ~

Oh . . . and I like quotes. You'll see a few as you read through.

This book isn't comprehensive by any means. There is a ton of good, related content out there. I've only outlined what I believe are the most important topics for you to consider. To help you focus even more on only what's important, anytime I made a suggestion for action, I attempted to categorize it into one of three buckets:

- Take it with a grain of salt
- Strong Suggestion
- Mandate

If I say that one of my ideas is just one data point, it means it's a personal philosophy I enjoy, but I don't feel too strongly about it. Take it with a grain of salt.

If I repeat a point several times in the book or use CAPITAL LETTERS to emphasize that point, it means this idea is the only way, don't do anything less. It's a mandate.

Anything that is not a mandate, or a single data point, is a strong suggestion from me. Means it's worked for me and many others, but I can see how other methods (that I haven't tried) may work as well.

To succeed . . .

More focus. Less noise. Bias towards action.

Good luck!

Table of Contents

1. To Win . . . shift more focus to your Social Life and Career

At the start of your journey, there are strong feelings of fear and excitement as you get ready to physically relocate to the U.S. Simple experiences like arriving at the airport, figuring out how to get to your hotel, watching people and thinking how different everything is, turn out to be memorable. If it was your choice to come to the U.S. (not heavily influenced by parents or outside factors), there will be emotions of fun and excitement as you arrive. You are on an adventure, after all.

Like with most international students, your first month will be about figuring out how to live alone. For the first time in your life, you will work on new chores like buying furniture for your room, signing up for a phone plan, and for many of us (like me), cooking for ourselves. This will be anxiety-inducing but a good way to stay busy initially. With everything being new, you will search for anchors to maintain some sense of stability in your life. Chatting with your family and friends from home will help, and believe it or not, confidence in your academic skills can be a strong anchor, keeping you grounded in your new world where everything has changed. Many will find themselves happy to dive into schoolwork.

Around the third month, you are more situated and you have a routine, which will naturally shift much of your attention to needing to connect with people. When your energy demands more human connection, take this as an opportunity to intentionally improve your "meeting new people" skills. For many, academics will be their primary focus and purpose through this time and until graduation. It will also be their excuse for not seeking social connections, why they didn't participate in non-school activities, and why they didn't push themselves to experience a little more of the American culture. After all, this (academics) is why they, why you, are here. It's what got you here and what will help you succeed in the next step of your life. Right?

It's normal to want to stick to what has made us successful so far. But to grow, we must learn something new by putting ourselves in situations that are unfamiliar and uncomfortable. It starts with your social life! Don't ignore your need to connect with others. Spend guilt-free time on it. It's an important part of your education.

You WILL experience some culture shock ... don't let it stop you

Let me share a bit of my story. My first year was very challenging when it came to meeting people. I gravitated towards the small group of students who grew up in the same country as I did. Should I hang out with them? I did. But I quickly felt I was missing out on the whole point of this experience. I wanted to make American friends, or generally any friends who were not where I was from. It was a big part of my drive to study in a new country. Though in theory finding a diverse set of friends was possible, the culture shock was real, and frequently demotivated me from trying. Speaking to Americans made me feel like I was on a totally different wavelength, and raised many self-doubts about my language skills and likeability. I found myself in many, many awkward conversations.

I learned that most American students tried to click or connect with each other by searching for something they have in common. A lot of conversations I overheard went something like this -

Yeah . . . I'm from Scranton, PA.

Oh cool, which high school did you go to?

West Scranton High.

My best friend's cousin went there, he played baseball.

Oh, what was his name?

Pete.

Yeah, I know Pete ...

Conversations I had with Americans went more like this -

Where are you from?

Oh . . . well . . . It's a long story but I grew up in the U.A.E.

What's that?

It's a country, ever heard of Dubai?

Oh yeah, are you like a prince?

No, not really . . .

Rarely did conversations evolve past that. I found that seven or eight out of ten Americans had little to no interest in meeting unfamiliar people. They were looking for similarities. They, too, are in unfamiliar, new territory and are looking for connectivity. Can you blame them?

However, two out of ten were genuinely interested in learning more about international students. With them, I felt that similarly to me, they left home searching for something different. I really enjoyed speaking with them and felt more included every time I did. Find these people, ignore the ones that don't engage.

Besides meeting potential friends, a huge part of the American college life revolves around interactions with the opposite sex. In my case, I was looking forward to meeting girls, to date and to make friends.

Like for most people, High School is not exactly satisfying in that department and university is an opportunity to start fresh. I was excited to get started. I heard that Penn State had mixed dorms, meaning the buildings had a floor of guys, then a floor of girls and so on. This was a big deal for me. I had a hard time grasping how this was possible. In my high school (late 90s), girls sat in one half of the class and guys in the other. You would get in trouble for sitting too close to a girl during breaks.

After much anticipation, I found out I was placed in the largest freshman dorm building (ten floors) on the east campus, and that it was all-male . . . Wonderful I thought ☹ . . . I could have stayed home and saved my parents tens of thousands of dollars for a similar experience.

I tried to meet girls in class and in the few parties I found myself invited to (or invited myself to). The story here is the same. Seven or eight out of ten girls had no interest in international backgrounds, they were looking for familiarity (which was not me). For the two girls that had interest, we would have a nice chat, but it never led to more. It took me a few years to really get better at this. I had a lot of inner work to do to get comfortable being my genuine self in all situations. I also needed to understand American culture better so I could build rapport more naturally. Most importantly, I needed to battle my constant fear of trying to meet new people.

Despite the initial setbacks you may face, I genuinely hope you don't miss out on the opportunity to socialize and connect with people while you are here. I encourage you to ask yourself: "Which activity will I learn and grow from more? Sticking solely with what has made me successful so far (academics) or trying to improve my social skills and integration in a new country?" For most of you, the latter will be key to your job hunting and career success.

Work on your career sooner rather than later ... get a head start

Towards the end of your first year, you'll hopefully have two or a handful of friends to spend time with. You will think about your long break from classes, and potentially anticipate what you want to do when classes start again. Whether you are an undergrad or grad, you should have planned for life's next step - your professional career. An internship, a co-op or a full-time role could be in your purview, depending on where you are in your pursuit of a degree. Most will not have a clue with how to start. Most will not have a lot of motivation to begin this phase either, still focusing on academics and thinking they'll figure it out when they need to. It's common to procrastinate on this subject. When you do get started, you'll quickly learn that the resources available to you (family or career center) don't have a clear roadmap for you to follow. You will have to take bits and pieces of advice from here and there, and figure out how to make them work for you. Buy yourself time and start working on your career early in your journey.

I'll admit this is easier said than done. I didn't think about work until I graduated (which was a terribly bad idea, please don't wait until then!). I struggled to get my first job and ultimately went back to the U.A.E., where I found a sales role (I graduated as an electrical engineer and this felt like a downgrade). After one and a half years, I made it back to the U.S. in a more technical role but had to accept an entry-level job despite having had some work experience.

If I could attribute this slip up to one reason, it would be that I expected to be guided into this new phase of getting a job. That was far from reality. University was much more unstructured than high school for me, both for academics and for career development. At American universities, you get what you put in, and you must be proactive about everything.

Like many schools across the globe, at my high school it was one structured step after the next: Study for your tests, go to external exam classes, take prep exams, schedule and take the external exam, apply to colleges, go to an essay writing class, write essays and review with your counselor, etc. . . . We basically didn't need to think, just do. While this structure is tremendous in helping us achieve great academic results, and with getting into global universities, it isn't the education we needed to succeed with integrating into a new culture, to adapt to unstructured environments, or to prepare for our careers. At university, you have to be proactive and own your career development.

It starts with going to your career guidance center and speaking to a counselor. I recall doing this once at Penn State and found the meeting to be useless, because the counselor didn't give me the exact steps I needed to take next (I was expecting exact steps). I then attended a networking session and didn't know what to do, stood around feeling silly. I went to a career development class and listened to them talk about how important networking is and to poor advice on how to network - like "smile" to become more likeable. They told me to write a S.M.A.R.T. resume. Not knowing back then that I had to manage my own job search and career path, I felt that the resume was the only positive thing I really got out of my university's career counseling services.

It didn't seem then that anyone had this "what to do after academics, how to find a good job for me" written down step by step. Today, even the top schools in the U.S. struggle to deliver a clear career map for international students. It's mostly on you to figure out the steps by speaking with your career counselor repeatedly, attending career sessions, taking notes and following whatever advice they give you. Even if it's not something that works for you personally.

You have to experiment, fail and learn, create your path, because that perfect structured roadmap isn't included in your tuition. My failure with not taking a strong first step in my career is on me, not on my school. What I do wish I had that wasn't available to me then was a mentor. Someone, family or not family, that could have told me and persisted that it was on me to be proactive about setting up for a successful career start. Someone, who like me, was an international student who succeeded with finding the right steps and who could have guided me with my specific questions and challenges. I also still wish the steps were written down. How hard can that really be?

This is what I'm hoping to do for you, why I've set up the "International Student Handbook". I want to get you access to the best international student career content, and to mentors who were international students and now have successful careers in the U.S. I believe in your potential to have a very successful career in the U.S. I want to encourage you to believe in yourself, and to take the appropriate steps to make that happen.

~Select stories from International Students

currently in this journey ~

Below are a few real-life stories of international students' experiences in the U.S., for you to get a flavor of what to expect from this journey. These students took the time to share their stories with me, so I can share them with you. They like the idea that their experience might in some way benefit other students just getting started. While each experienced their journeys differently, they all have two things in common - they are down to earth, nice people – and they want to Win! Two qualities you can never go wrong with!

AN - Ho Chi Minh City, Vietnam - Bachelors in Finance

I moved to the U.S. at 19, just after graduating from high school. I've only ever lived with my parents until then, and wasn't allowed to travel anywhere alone. No school camping trips, or staying overnight anywhere. As a family, we didn't travel much, not even within Vietnam. So, going to the U.S., alone, was a big deal. I started at a community college and stayed at a Vietnamese home-stay the first few months. Being amongst other Vietnamese allowed me to adapt at my pace. The biggest thing I noticed when I started classes was that students spoke very freely. They say what's on their mind. I listened, avoided speaking so I wouldn't say the wrong thing. In Vietnam, if I know something, I say it. In the US, I lost a bit of that confidence, especially in front of groups. But participation was 20% of my grade, and I had to do something. There was this one professor (from English class) that encouraged us to speak up. He was patient when students answered his questions. He made us feel comfortable but also gave us feedback on how we could have said things better. The more I understood the language and the culture, the more confident I felt. I also learned that I don't need to be 100% right every time I speak. I can say what's on my mind, and it doesn't have to be perfect. Americans do that naturally.

I was motivated to integrate more and looked for jobs on campus. I'd search for anything; reception work, cleaning dishes, tutoring. I went to every department and asked if I could volunteer. I didn't need to get paid, just wanted to learn. I ended up volunteering at the gym and worked my way up to getting paid to handle the reception area. I also tutored adult learners (immigrants in their 40s, 50s), taught them English out of all things. This helped develop my language skills a lot and gave me a great foundation that set me up for challenges in the future. I felt fortunate initially that a few American students at work took their time when speaking with me, to help me through conversations. Americans are great at small talk and can speak about any topic. Five years into this journey, and I'm much better at small talk myself. I'm more comfortable now with being myself in class or in a working environment. I'm still working through figuring out what I should and shouldn't talk about with personal topics, particularly in the work environment. Not sure what the boundaries are. I'm getting there.

LI - Shanghai, China - Masters in Analytics

I feel I am generally too warm-hearted and open. Soon after I arrived in the U.S., I moved in with two Chinese roommates. Naturally, I tried starting conversations to build a relationship with them, but they didn't want to talk much or share things. I guess they were suspicious of how forward I was and nervous to be alone in the U.S. themselves. I wanted to connect, so I cooked some food for us, but they refused to eat it. We lived together for four months, and they warmed up to me as the time passed by. Generally, it was difficult for me to connect with other Chinese students. I'm from a modest family. I heard most Chinese students in the U.S. came from wealthy families. So, I naturally tried to mingle with non-Chinese. It's not that I didn't want to hang out with them, more that we typically had a different set of values. I mingled with students from India during the first semester. They were friendly, and we shared similar traits like hard work.

I was looking to earn some money on campus. My first job was to help undergrad students adapt to their first year at college. I organized events for them. They were young, 18 and 19. I helped connect them with others who had gone through the same experience. I volunteered as well. For book festivals, community service, etc. It was an American-Chinese girl who introduced me to volunteering. She was a military student, and came across as highly disciplined with her time, and yet so nice to everyone she met! She gets up at 5 am for training, then gets to her academic work through the afternoon, then a part-time job, then goes out at night. How can a person have that much energy? She would encourage me all the time, especially to be more open, which was tough for me as an international student and as a woman (because of my culture). Because of her, I joined our school's dancing club to meet new friends, and even participated in a Spartan race in 2018. I was a weak girl before I went to the U.S. Now, I am a two-Spartan-Races finisher, and I enjoy working out. I think we clicked because she still had some of the Chinese culture inside, which helped us relate. We are still friends.

PAM - Guangzhou (Canton), China - Masters in Project Management

I've been in the U.S. for three years, and came here after completing my bachelor's degree in China. The biggest change I experienced initially was that I had to handle everything on my own. When I graduated from my bachelors, I worked for three years before starting my U.S. journey. Living with my parents while working, I spent most of what I earned on things I wanted (not needed). I also didn't have to worry about food, chores at home ... that all changed in the U.S. While I had many challenges, including integrating with the new culture, I was happy to have them. I wanted to be out of my comfort zone. But even simple things were not straightforward anymore. For example, when I would order food at the food court, I didn't know the polite way to do that. In China, you just say, "I want this, I want that". Here, you say, "Hi, may I have this, and that". Despite being a friendly and outgoing person, I had to think before I spoke, more often than I was used to. But I needed my friends circle, so language wasn't going to stop me. After 5 months, I had friends and built a good relationship with my academic advisor. It didn't take me long to adapt.

During my internship, discussing work topics helped bridge the connection gap with Americans. The work environment forced me to quickly learn a lot of language and cultural nuances, and have heard from other international students that their work experience helped them in a similar way. I'm in a full-time role now. I had to apply 1000 times before I found it. I focused on LinkedIn by following the companies I wanted to work for, and connecting with people who worked there. The job I found was through searching for "analyst" roles on LinkedIn. I would do that frequently, and one time, saw that a recruiter had posted a role. The role wasn't with one of my target companies, nevertheless, I applied right away (by sending the recruiter a message through LinkedIn) and got a call back. The recruiter said I would be a good fit. She set up calls with hiring managers in the company, and the interviews went well. I then met with my future manager in person, who thought I was a good fit as well, leading to them sending me an offer. The whole process took two weeks. It was definitely a great opportunity. It gave me a chance to stay here to get experience and bought me time to further explore my career goals and plan accordingly. Recently, my company has been giving me a lot of opportunities to learn by sending me to training programs, so I like them more and more.

KETAN - Delhi, India - Masters in Engineering Management

After my bachelors, I worked for a small company that designed piping for manufacturing industries. We had inefficiencies that could have benefited from better management, so when it came time to think about my masters, I was motivated to focus on a management degree. I chose the U.S. as I felt that is where good management was prized. I've been here a little over a year now, and admittedly was very scared when I first arrived. When I look back now, I feel very lucky. Somehow many people came to help me along the way. On my first visa interview prior to leaving India, I got rejected. I had little confidence my second one would go better. This put me in a difficult situation as orientation and classes were about to start, but I hadn't heard back on my visa status. I had a cousin who told me that orientation was really important, because of the people you meet and the groups you form. I missed all that. My visa was ultimately accepted, and I flew over after classes started. Although I missed a few classes, my professors had kept me up to date with assignments. I arrived feeling the odds of this being a successful journey were already off to a bad start. I had also never lived alone. During undergrad, and while I worked in India, I lived with my parents. So, all of this was pressure. Somehow, it's been working for me, though. When I got here, my roommates helped a ton. They gave me a tour, showed me how to get to my classes.

I've always felt socially awkward, not open to speaking with people. I'm doing better because I decided to improve. I pushed myself to get over this in the U.S., especially so I don't miss out on opportunities that come my way. I took it a step at a time, and it has boosted my confidence. I'm in a co-op now, which in my opinion is the best way to develop your skills with interacting with others. My manager is amazing. He pushes me to get better on every aspect (soft and hard skills). My big personal focus continues to be on improving my interactions with others, now that I've started to see some success with it, I know I will just get better and better.

My goal is to be a full-time employee in the US. I've been learning data science, and want to go down that route in some way. My plan is to stay in the U.S. for at least three to four years before I go back to India, to put my knowledge to use there. Here, the transparency and feedback in American work culture have helped push me and polish my skills. In India, the political part of work would hold me back. I'd rather focus on my knowledge and skills, and how to take my ideas and work through them (which I feel is not possible in India at junior levels). I like the company I work for now so much; I want to work with them full time. I graduate at my 2-year mark, and if they don't offer me a role by then, I plan to extend my graduation date to keep searching for a job.

MANUELA - Mexico City, Mexico - Masters in Marketing Communications

I grew up dreaming about leaving my country, mostly because I didn't feel like I fit in. I had spent the first few years of my life in the U.S., so when I went back to Mexico and my family maintained the U.S. connection via access to American T.V. channels, I yearned to be a part of the full American culture. My desire to go to the U.S. only strengthened as I became a teenager and struggled to fit in, thinking I would probably feel more at home somewhere else. I finally got my wish to go abroad in college and went to Canada as an exchange student.

This experience opened my eyes and made me realize how not-American/Anglo I actually was. Part of it had to do with the fact that I come from a pretty conservative catholic family. When I went to my first Canadian college party, I realized that I didn't fit in here either and that I had to make a choice. Adopt parts of a foreign culture to remain relevant or be true to my upbringing and culture. I chose both. I kept my conservative way of thinking in terms of my own actions. However, I made a point of making sure that I did not judge those around me who were more liberal. Part of what helped me through this transition was a vibrant international exchange student community, where students were in the same boat as me. Though tempted, I refused to just hang out with the Latin community and made friends with people from Brazil, Germany, Spain, Norway, France, Australia and Japan.

When I returned to Mexico, I realized I wanted to leave but not for the same reasons. I felt more comfortable in my own skin and wanted to experience more cultures and see more of the world. That led me to a year and a half of working in Belgium in which I experienced life in a totally different environment. Adapting again was not easy, but after some time, I got used to the European way of life, while keeping my core beliefs. With Brussels being an international hub, I made friends with people from Tanzania, Poland, Malaysia, Morocco, Turkey, India, Portugal, Ukraine, Greece and Finland.

At this point, it would have been hard for me to go back to a life in a bubble in Mexico, where people only know and understand one way of thinking. My experience just made me hungry to continue to explore and learn more. My life working in Europe, helped me realize something I hadn't contemplated before. I really did want to live in the U.S.

To do this, I decided I wanted to do my master's degree as a pathway towards a green card. I got into the school I wanted and set forth on living my childhood dream: studying and living in the U.S.

I will admit that having lived in Europe just before made it a little bit hard for me to get used to American culture. I wasn't used to people smiling at each other every day, asking how they are and giving the canned response of "fine." In a way, it felt a bit fake, having just arrived from a more melancholic (European) culture in which brutal honesty is pretty much the norm. In this circumstance, I tried melting as much as I could with the Americans in my class but struggled with finding enough common ground to create deep connections. I realized that deep connections in the U.S. are quite hard to forge. Meanwhile, everyone was simply pleasant and smiling at each other, working side by side, guided by small talk. I yearned for connection and again, I came to drift towards the international community. This time I fully embraced the Latin culture and connected with people from Costa Rica, Puerto Rico, Panama and Peru. I had always tried up to that point to mix with cultures clearly different to my own. My time with the Latin community helped me realize the differences within the Latin world. These connections also helped me land a job in the U.S. that eventually led to my getting a work visa and meeting my husband (thanks to the connections of a Panamanian friend looking to hire someone with my background). I got lucky.

2. Who do you want to become, and what will you do to get there?

*"**Your beliefs** become your thoughts, Your thoughts become your words,*

Your words become your actions, Your actions become your habits,

*Your habits become your values, Your values **become your destiny***"

~ Mahatma Gandhi ~

If you read only one chapter from this book, make sure it's this one. Succeeding starts with adopting the right mindset. I've accumulated thoughts on what that mindset is, coming from years of study, practice, failures, and learnings. The framework I've outlined is meant to help you figure out who you are, where you want to go and who you want to be. This will help you beyond your career ambitions, it extends to all parts of your life.

My objective is to make you aware of basic personal development and growth concepts, and my hope is that you take action on these concepts afterwards. It's likely, however, that over 90% of readers will not make a real effort to change their mindsets. They won't because it's hard and because it's not a priority at the moment. You need clarity of mind with what you want to do next with your life (in the near term, at least), to take real action. Very few have that clarity in these early stages of their professional lives and that's normal. If you feel this way, jump to the last section in this chapter, *"Your purpose is unique to you, search for it"*. If you have never picked up a self-help book or read about personal development concepts, keep reading. Make yourself aware of these basic concepts.

If you skim through this material and feel you have it down already, I encourage you to keep practicing these concepts regularly.

Ready to dive into actionable career steps and job searching techniques? Skip this wishy-washy inner game stuff, and jump to the later chapters. Just remember there isn't a magic bullet to finding a job . . . it's starts with getting yourself in order first.

As you read through, remember to be kind to yourself and to like yourself, regardless of where you are in your journey.

Adopt a Growth Mindset

Every experience you have and how you perceive that experience affects your mindset. For example, the first time I tried coding in undergrad, I was discouraged and thought I could never get good at it. Coding was difficult, but that wasn't what threw me off, as I'm always ready to take on difficult challenges. What got to me was seeing others in my class excel at it right away (because they were naturally good or they had previous experience). I didn't give myself a chance to get better. The thought that I was behind, that others were already excelling at it, dropped my confidence. I realized later that wanting to be good at coding is easy, anyone can want to be good at anything. I had no solid reason for trying, so I convinced myself to not bother. I gave up too easily.

Thinking back on my life, I found many instances like this, which ***made me develop a mindset of "there are certain things I can't do".*** This is called a "fixed mindset". That mindset crushed my hopes of wanting to improve my skills in many areas, and of achieving certain goals, often before I even started trying. My personal reason usually was that I didn't like feeling inferior, behind or not as good as I thought I was. The other reason was simply not believing it was possible, which was what made me afraid to try. My list included: scuba diving, philosophy, chess, Tekken, travelling on my own, speaking in public, meeting new people, asking someone out, becoming a millionaire, starting my own company, among others. Some I can say I've overcome, while some I am still working on. What is your list?

Think about the opposite of the above. What in your life did you excel at, despite not being naturally good at it, or fearing it? Why did you do it and how did you muster up energy to keep at it until you excelled? - Your mom threatening to beat you with her slipper doesn't count ☺.

For me, that example was soccer. In high school, I was definitely not the most skillful player, I was average at best. Growing up, I was obsessed with soccer, but rarely did I get picked to play for the school team. Yet somehow, I was team captain the last three years of high school. I played every lunch break, I attended every extra P.E. practice session, I played at home, etc. I loved to play. **_The reason I succeeded was that I wanted to_**. I had a great desire for it and I wanted to be the best. I had purpose. Look back at your stories and see if that resonates. Purpose allows us to channel all available energy we have to a single objective. In physics, energy cannot be created nor destroyed, it transfers from one medium to another. In you, your energy is also finite, but it's being consumed by multiple priorities. What if you channeled it all meaningfully to achieve your goals? Imagine what you can do.

Having a fixed mindset blocks you from sending energy to an activity, killing any chance of you improving your skills or attaining your goals. A fixed mindset convinces you that you can't get good at something (it's too hard), that trying will make you feel bad or affect your self-esteem negatively. It leads you to believe that it's not worth your time, that it's impossible to achieve or progress on your skills. In these cases, **you have convinced yourself that you can't make it happen** (like my coding example).

It's important to be aware that your mindset, your perception of the situation, is what's blocking you . . . not your actual ability to succeed.

Here is a definition of growth mindset from Carol Dwek, Professor at Stanford University: "***In a growth mindset, people believe that their most basic abilities can be developed through dedication and hard work*** - brains and talent are just the starting point. This view creates a love of learning and a resilience that is essential for great accomplishment. Virtually all great people have had these qualities."

If I believe Prof. Dwek, I can direct energy to improve myself. Someone with a growth mindset believes they can do anything they put their mind to, by adopting the idea that they can learn anything when they dedicate enough time (and energy) to it. They believe they can change, intentionally, to become the person they want to be. You are constantly evolving, growing, changing, whether you are doing it intentionally or not. If you believe that you can become the person you want to be, you will. If you don't believe you can grow into the person you want to be (whatever your desire may be), I want you to think about where else you are channeling your energy. Remember, your energy isn't going anywhere. If your energy isn't being intentionally directed, it's likely lackadaisically being directed to activities that are meaningless to you (like reading your junk mail frequently, checking Instagram excessively) or worse, it's being directed negatively to make you feel bad about yourself (e.g., thinking "I'll never get the job I want, I wish it could just happen for me already" . . . it's easy to wish that, but thinking that way too frequently is a misuse of your energy). There is a wealth of free information on Fixed vs. Growth mindsets online, do yourself a favor and read up on it. Keep educating yourself on this topic until you adopt a growth mindset.

The first step in changing your mindset is to be aware that you CAN, and then to gather information on what a better mindset looks like. To actually do it is a beast of a challenge. The remaining parts of this chapter discuss the building blocks needed to adopt a growth mindset. I can make you aware of how to go about it, but you have to take action and step through this journey to make it reality.

Discover your Self-Limiting Beliefs

Eben Pagan, successful entrepreneur, wrote, *"If you tell yourself something enough times, you'll begin to BELIEVE it*. This new belief will take on a mind of its own and start creating its own self-talk. Most people who have negative beliefs also have negative self-talk that creates a self-fulfilling prophecy." I was 18 when I first read this, and it was the first time this concept was ever pointed out to me.

Like many 18-year-olds, particularly those who have ventured off to university in a different country, I had many self-doubts. I was self-conscious about how likable I was, about my conversation skills, etc. This list turns out to be similar amongst international students. If you have self-doubts, it's likely many of your peers have those exact same insecurities. You are not alone. Your self-limiting beliefs are related to what you want from life. For example, "I can't get a job in a start-up in the U.S. because they won't sponsor me" or "I can't make friends with Americans because I've tried and it's too hard" or "No point in talking to that girl I like because she won't be interested in me". Think about what you want, and if you have not gone after it wholeheartedly, ask yourself if you actually don't care about it that much OR if you have a self-limiting belief preventing you from trying. Write those beliefs down. The clearer you can be about your self-limiting belief, the better.

When I was younger, I had self-esteem issues (for example, I didn't like what I looked like). Battling through these issues took years to overcome. I always knew I had them, I just never knew that I could do anything to change my beliefs and improve my confidence. You CAN. If you can relate to any of the above, I urge you to work on it NOW, not later. Here is what you can do to overcome self-limiting beliefs.

I will say it again and again because this is paramount – first, write down your self-limiting beliefs so you are aware they exist.

Recognize as you are writing them they are your own "perception" of the situation, not reality. They are your mental "interpretation" about yourself. The best thing about "perceptions" and "interpretations" you have about yourself is that YOU HAVE THE POWER to guide them. *You can't change how others think, perceive, or interpret you until you change how you view yourself.* And to do that is a choice.

Next, decide that you want to change. If a current (self-limiting) belief you have is not useful to you today or in the future, you can (and should) work on changing it. It won't be easy, it will take time, but it will be totally worth it! How to do that is through positive self-talk. "If you tell yourself something enough times, you'll begin to BELIEVE it". This is true whether you say negative or positive things to yourself.

Adjust your Self-Talk

"THE WOLF YOU FEED"

*One evening an old Cherokee told his grandson about **a battle that goes on inside people**.*

He said, "My son, the battle is between two "wolves" inside us all.

***One is Evil.** It is anger, envy, jealousy, sorrow, regret, greed, arrogance, self-pity, guilt, resentment, inferiority, lies, false pride, superiority, and ego.*

***The other is Good.** It is joy, peace, love, hope, serenity,*

26

humility, kindness, benevolence, empathy, generosity, truth, compassion and faith."

*The grandson thought about it for a minute and then asked his grandfather: "**Which wolf wins?**"*

*The old Cherokee simply replied, "**The one you feed.**"*

~ unknown origin ~

The first time I read about "autosuggestion" was in the famous business book "Think and Grow Rich" by Napoleon Hill. The gist of this term is about talking to yourself positively. Napoleon Hill wrote a whole chapter on this. Others have written whole books.

If you've never heard of autosuggestion, here is the dictionary definition: Autosuggestion - the hypnotic or subconscious adoption of an idea that one has originated within oneself, e.g., through repetition of verbal statements to oneself in order to change behavior.

It sounds complicated, but all it's saying is that if you say something to yourself enough times, you will believe it. This phenomenon is true whether you say negative or positive things to yourself, and whether you intentionally control what you say to yourself or just let your mind run with whatever it comes up with. *Your mind doesn't discriminate or care. It takes the input, and if that input is repeated consistently (whether it's positive or negative), your mind will bake it into your subconscious. Those thoughts then become beliefs hard to shake.*

How do you talk to yourself all day? Negatively or positively? Knowing that what you say to yourself consistently will become a belief that's hard to shake, can you see how destructive it is to harbor negative self-talk? It's really no different than eating unhealthy food or smoking. If you do it too frequently, and for a long period, you will spoil your health and it will take time to break that habit and regain your original healthy self. If you talk negatively to yourself, you will spoil your mind.

You may be thinking this sounds hard (and I like burgers and having a smoke sometimes). It is hard, nothing good is easy. It's like going to the gym. It will take time for you to ramp up and build the habit of enjoying this exercise, and then see the fruit of your labor. Here is how you can get started.

First, pay attention to what you say to yourself, especially the negative self-talk.

Examples:

"I'm not good looking enough to find someone attractive" -

"If I speak up in class, I'll sound stupid" -

"No point of trying to network with others at a career fair because I don't know what to say or what the point is anyway" -

Whatever your negative self-talk sentences are, write them down.

It's unlikely you are intentionally saying any of these things to yourself, so don't freak out about what they are, or become overly conscious about them. Just be aware of them, and what situations usually trigger them. Mark down the thoughts you would like to change first.

Next, for each thought, ask yourself if it is useful to you, and how you might reframe it to be more neutral or positive. Write down the specific thing you would like to say to yourself instead.

Let's look at this example:

"If I speak up in class, I'll sound stupid".

Ok. Is that thought useful to you? If you think that in every class, you probably won't say anything all semester (even though you want to). It's also likely that your perception of yourself is false, and that more than a few people in the class would benefit from what you want to say or find it insightful (not stupid).

What are some ways you might re-frame this thought?

You could try:

"I'm afraid of speaking up in class" - This is better than calling yourself "stupid".

Or

"I want to speak up, but I'm afraid" -

With this, you are reminding yourself that you have a desire to speak up even though it's scary.

When we compare "If I speak up in class I'll sound stupid" to "I want to speak up, but I'm afraid", notice how it shifts your thinking to your wanting to do it (desire is a powerful motivator) but fear is stopping you (fear is something you can address). If you think you will sound stupid when speaking, that would likely completely block you from trying and will affect your long-term self-image. Avoid the word stupid and others like it. Try to shift to words like it's "hard" or you have "fear" or you want to do something but "don't know how to". You can work with those thoughts by addressing fear and focusing on building new skills. More on that next.

Fear is Part of the Process

You've been overcoming it your whole life. Learning to walk and swim. Going to school for the first time and taking your first external exam. Presenting to an audience for the first time (and your upcoming presentation is just as scary, right?). Living alone for the first time, your mom's shoe thrown at you (typical hazard in Middle Eastern countries), and so on.

Disclaimer: I don't condone any sort of violence. It's just that the shoe is an imminent threat to misbehaving kids in the Middle East, but one that children later as adults realize comes from their parents' deep love for them. Either way, the parents must be stopped by all means necessary ☺.

__Literally, no progress would have been made in your life without your ability to overcome fear__, which you have done time and time again even if you don't give yourself credit for it.

Next time you experience fear, think of what's the worst that can go wrong? 99.9% of the time the worst thing that can happen is made up in your head and not a reality, especially in your academic, professional or social life. In these contexts, you are not in situations of imminent physical threat. It's important to say this again, *__your worst fears in these contexts are fantasies made up in your head__*. Often, you are not conscious that you are creating these fantasies. They are an automatic reaction and a result of letting your mind run free based on your emotion of fear.

I'm suggesting you take control of every moment you feel fear by doing two things:

1. Asking yourself insightful questions about what you are feeling

2. Preparing to take action ahead of the moment that causes the fear

Next time you fear taking action, ask yourself these questions:

• How would I rate my fear in this situation vs. any other situation I experience fear with?

• What is the worst that can happen?

• What is the long-term outcome of not taking action and how will that make me feel?

Let's go back to the example of fearing speaking in class. We have now reframed our negative self-talk to be more neutral - "I want to speak up, but I'm afraid". Get a sense of how afraid you are each time you want to speak up in class. Some days you are more tired than others or have thoughts or priorities taking up your mind space, and your energy is low. Sometimes you are refreshed and feel ready to take on the world. Your perception of how afraid you are will be different depending on how you are feeling and your energy at that moment. Take that into account.

Next, think about what's the worst that can happen. Think about outcomes that are realistic, not things like "your professor or peers will think worse of you". What they and others think is something you will never know about unless they tell you, so it's none of your business or concern. Let it go! A more realistic outcome might be someone commenting on what you said, potentially pointing out an error with what you said or disagreeing with you. A less likely, but realistic outcome, might be that the class laughs at what you said or the way you said it.

How would that make you feel? Would it be the end of the world? Can you let it roll off your shoulder and move on, thinking this was a good learning experience instead? Those examples are the worst possible realistic outcomes. Nothing more. To dig deep and find motivation through fear, think about the long-term impact of you not speaking up in this class or in others. When you graduate and start work, do you think you will have to speak at meetings? To present in front of groups? The answer is a definite yes. 100%. The stakes are higher than in a university lecture room. Do you really want to wait until the pressure is way up to speak in a room full of people? . . . or is this low-risk environment at a university a more appropriate venue to practice? Think about how not acting now, knowing that it's important for your future, will make you feel now. Anytime you experience fear of action, find something inside you, that motivates you to take action in the moment. Make up a reason, create a story in your head, about why it's important to take action now. It takes work, but it's worth it.

Despite any advice from me or motivation you can muster for yourself, fear can be debilitating sometimes. Some situations will make you feel extreme anxiety and fear, and it won't be the last time you feel this emotion as part of your career or social life. Every time I have to present to a group of people more senior than I, it's the worst moment of my life. I feel debilitating fear. The kind where I want to quit my job to avoid these situations. Every time. I'm at the point where I can anticipate that I will feel that way and prepare for it, both of which help reduce my anxiety, but they don't eliminate my fear. The most important thing in those situations is to not let your lack of action (if you choose to avoid these situations) or any outcome, affect your self-image. If you are in a growth mindset, this is all part or the process. It's not about who you are today, it's this moment being a part of becoming who you want to be. Don't internalize negative outcomes. Use them to learn, and move on.

Preparation is key here. It won't necessarily eliminate or reduce the fear before the big moment, but during the moment, it will give you strength. Going back to our example of fear of speaking in class, one way to prepare is to come up with something you want to say before the class even starts. My favorite way to make sure I say something in any meeting is to prepare a question in advance. Think about what topics will be discussed in class, prepare a question, and find the right moment for you to ask it. Just do it. Over time with this kind of attitude (and the strategies above), not only will you become more comfortable, you will thrive.

Note: I've used the example of being afraid to speak up in class to stay consistent. Please insert your examples of what you fear and apply the same framework.

Focus on Skills

*"You miss **100 percent** of the shots you never take"*

~ Wayne Gretzky, Ice Hockey Legend ~

If you haven't noticed already, the objective of the above sections, from Growth Mindset to dealing with Fear, is to orient you to shift your focus and energy to building SKILLS. Skills you need to become successful. Each person will have a different starting point for each essential skill. The suggestions in the above sections are hard to implement, especially when you are just starting to learn about them. I want to try, as best as possible, to describe what it feels like when you get good at adopting a growth mindset.

When you are good, you will easily, effortlessly, get out of your own way to allow yourself to learn a skill and grow. You will face your fears and be indifferent to the outcome of any situation, because you know it's part of the growth process. You will intentionally direct your energy and focus on building the skills you need. You will LIKE yourself. You will like yourself regardless of your starting point with any skill, regardless of the self-limiting beliefs and negative self-talk you want to overcome, regardless of the fear of trying that you have. You will like yourself because as part of this growth process, you have permission to make missteps, to fall down, to fail. You will be kind to yourself when those things happen (and they will) because you understand that they reflect you pushing to become the person you want to be. They reflect your courage and your desire. You will feel you have come a long way by succeeding academically and traveling and living in a new country. Most importantly, you will remember to celebrate the small wins along the way. These wins - anything from cooking your own meals, speaking up in class, to connecting better with strangers, to landing an internship or full-time role - small or big - reinforce the positive self-talk and beliefs you are trying to adopt, and make you better and better. Don't wait to try.

The key skills I emphasize for career success are writing and networking, both being forms of communication. We will cover those topics in more detail later. ***For now, understand what*** *it takes to build any skill: Energy, Focus, Dedication and Time.*

Building career skills or social skills do not differ from learning to play tennis, a new video game or how to dance. **You will suck at the beginning**. Why doesn't it bother us that much when it's tennis? We have a tendency of beating ourselves up when the skill involves connecting with other people. We think that we should already be good at that, and if we aren't, then something is wrong with us. Not true. It's just our ego blocking us from learning this skill.

So, I'll ask this:

Can you become good at tennis or dancing from the first lesson?

Can you learn to drive a car by reading a book?

Will asking your career advisor about how to network make you good at it?

Those are all pieces that help you learn, but to get good, you need to prioritize learning and practicing those skills and dedicate enough time (consistently every week) to them. International students are often good with prioritizing time and energy for academics. I've mentioned this once, but it's worth mentioning again. A lot of students' success so far stems from their academic efforts, and students typically believe that continuing to focus much of their energy on academics will lead to success with their professional careers. This is not true, nor is it a useful belief to have. I can say that with much confidence. ***You will have to get good at working with people.*** And to do that, you must shift to building those softer skills.

These skills include (but are not limited to):
- Networking (building rapport with strangers, small talk, etc.)
- Writing
- Presenting in public
- Selling (your ideas)
- Maintaining Relationships
- Working in groups
- Mentoring
- Coaching

Are you dedicating any time to these skills today? If you are, are they a priority and are you truly advancing? Or are they just something you need to get done, or time passing activities?

These skills are more important to your success now than ever. Shift from a complete focus on academics to a balance of academics and soft people skills. Make time if you have to, take them seriously and practice.

A quick point on Introverts

I feel for the people reading this who consider themselves introverts because I am one as well. The best public speaking teacher I've worked with is an introvert. All that means is that we naturally get more energy with quiet time vs. through being with people. We like our space to think, reflect, or do absolutely nothing if needed. We also, similarly to everyone else, like recognition from people and want to connect with others. We just don't like to do it all the time. There is a spectrum for Introversion to Extroversion and people fall in all parts of that spectrum. Knowing who you are and what gives you energy (vs. consumes it) is important. But wherever you fall in that spectrum, know that you can build the skills you need to succeed, regardless of how big of an introvert you consider yourself to be. Do yourself a favor and google successful introverts. You will find people like Elon Musk and Mahatma Gandhi, both with immense communication skills. Don't hold yourself back by using this as an excuse. More importantly, don't forget to like yourself throughout all this process. You will see improvement, that's the rewarding part. It's worth the effort.

Be Mindful of your Energy

I've referred to "energy" enough for you to notice. This section is about learning what gives you vs. drains your mental energy and how to direct it wisely to help you achieve your daily goals. As you go about your day, even though you may notice how your mental energy levels are doing, you may not be consciously using this information to your advantage. Let me explain.

Sometimes I feel like I want to talk to people, sometimes I don't.

Sometimes I'm ready and excited to play soccer, sometimes not (even though soccer is at the same time and day every week). Sometimes I feel just right to take a test. Other times I feel I can't get past the first question. Sometimes I'm more than able to listen and participate in class; other times, I can't stand listening to one more word. There are different physical and mental reasons you feel good about something one time and not so good the next. Did you get enough sleep? Have you had your coffee? Have you gotten any exercise? Those are examples of the physical reasons. All of which you can and should control. If you are used to having coffee in the morning, get your coffee before you do anything school or career-related in the morning. If you are not used to exercising, and you go for an 8-hour hike, don't have anything too important to do when you are back that day.

The mental and emotional reasons are more complicated, but also controllable through practice. Think of what activity you can do almost all day without losing mental energy (an activity that might even give you mental energy)? For some, it's being with people. For others, it's playing video games or reading. It doesn't matter what activity it is . . . It matters what it does for YOU. If studying or practicing English drains you, notice it. If solving tough applied math problems makes you lose track of time (because you enjoy it), notice it. ***Keep track of what GIVES you energy and what DRAINS your energy***. Literally make a list.

Here is how you use this information. If practicing or studying

English drains your energy (but it's still super important for your future), make sure you are doing it when you have maximum energy. Don't do it if you haven't gotten enough sleep, or your morning coffee. Don't do it right after taking a test. Do it when you feel ready for it, when you have energy for it, because it's important. Additionally, don't do it for too long at a time. It's no different than exercising. If you run for an hour, typically you will need a break. If you do a mental exercise that drains your energy, take a break when you must. Do something else during that break that gives you energy. If you have a big presentation, or an interview, or career networking event . . . unless you are an expert in performing in each, they will drain your energy. They will because they are new experiences and because they are new skills you are trying to build. You should expect that they will drain your energy and plan accordingly. Be ready physically (coffee, sleep, etc.) and don't have mentally draining activities right before the big moments. If an activity gives you mental energy, like talking to someone you care about, reading, or spending time outside alone in your thoughts, do it before these big moments. ***Manage your energy***.

The true need for energy management doesn't start until your first job (co-op, internship, or full-time role). When you have to be in an office for 8 to 9 hours at a time, and you are expected to perform. Can you imagine if all of those hours were spent doing something that drains your energy? For me, writing updates on the work my team has completed drains me. But it's super important because it accounts for our accomplishments and because my boss's boss's boss reads it. So, I need to do it well. What I do to make sure my updates are pristine is block my calendar for the first thing in the morning (when I have the most energy) and make sure I get it done then. If I sense my energy is drained while working on the update, I'll take a break, and take a copy of what I've written so far to show a colleague for feedback (talking to others gives me energy, especially when I've been working at my desk for an hour or so). When I have a big presentation to the senior leadership team, I can't control what time of the day that meeting takes place, so I manage my energy in a different way. I block time first thing in the morning to practice my presentation (use my best energy to feel good about my content). I'll make sure I don't have a heavy lunch that day. And finally, I'll block 30 mins before the meeting to make sure I collect my thoughts, regain any energy I've used up throughout the day (usually by taking a walk or talking to someone about non-work topics, both of which give me energy).

If you think this all sounds ridiculous, it's because it is. I'm with you. I struggled to get to a point where I understood the importance of this. I'm now more aware of what activities are my most important each day, and I plan for them so that I can put my best foot forward every time. It's not perfect, and I'm not perfect, but this process is solid and will make you leaps and bounds ahead of your peers not doing it. Come back to this section when you land that job.

Your Purpose is Unique to you, Search for it

Why? Why? WHY?

What's the point? So much effort is spent, and anxiety experienced in our lives. Often it doesn't seem like it's advancing your life in any way. It's certainly unclear if anything will ever be worth it, especially when you are just getting started with something (new school, new country, new job, etc.). Why are we putting ourselves through all this? Did we choose it? OR is it expected of us? The worst feeling ever is when we put ourselves through something because of someone else's expectations (Dad, Mom, society, etc.). Initially, especially early in our University and Professional lives, others' expectations are often the reason we are even here. We are following the standard path of life in the 21st century.

I feel that if you are still reading this, you are searching for something. You are not sure what it is exactly, but you are in the process (a lifelong one) of discovering it. You have hopes for your future, but you might have some questions on whether they can become reality, or if they are even the right hopes and dreams for you. So much of what others think still influences your choices. It's true for all of us. *My goal from this section is to help you drown out all the other noise in your life so you can listen more clearly to yourself,* to get closer to your purpose. I'm breaking down the process as it happened for me, and I'll caution that my take on purpose is only one data point (as is all the advice above on growth mindsets) that you should consider with other info you gather related to this topic.

Society

You are a part of it. If you are able, you need to contribute. There are people with disabilities who are not able, and a good society will look to take care of them. If you are able but don't contribute, you will become disabled. You will watch other people surpass you with their achievements and recognitions, and it will affect your self-esteem negatively (to the point of disability in some cases).

I am a big sci-fi fan. Some of my favorites are Star Trek and Battlestar Galactica. These shows intrigue me not because of the futurism as much as the societal lessons they provide. If thousands of humans are on one ship together in the middle of space, that's a society. They will have the same challenges as people on earth. Additionally, each needs to contribute as per their abilities, otherwise, the whole ship will fail. There is no escaping work, career, responsibilities if you are part of a society and are able. As you grow out of your home and leave your parents or caregivers, you will slowly but surely need to give back to the world (not just consume). You are part of society, and your purpose will be related to how you give back to it (through your work, career, lifelong mission).

A note on Money: Wanting more money is a goal. It's not a purpose. Confusing the two may lead to negative contributions to society (read about the Opioid crisis pharmaceutical companies created in the U.S.). It's great to work and aspire to make more money (and you should). Ideally, it will be through positive contributions to society, and even more ideally, it's aligned with your purpose.

Experimentation

Follow your desires to discover what you like and what you are good at. Try to discover what you don't like (often more important than discovering what you like) and what you are not good at (but need to get better at to develop your future). If you are studying Computer Science, it might be because you excelled at Math and Physics. If you are studying Business, it could be because you enjoy working with people. Sometimes, people study computer science or business because they think they should, not because their own desires led them there. It's ok, regardless of which bucket you fall into. Here is what matters.

You have been studying your whole life, and the workplace differs greatly from school. So regardless of what your major is, get as much work experience as you can during your university years. Get as much diverse social experience as you can. Go out! Even if you are not having fun in the beginning, do it. Experience it. Interact with others who are not like you. *(but always, please remember to be safe and trust your gut if you get into an uncomfortable situation).* Learn and grow from each experience. Push yourself with your job and career hopes. Get an internship, a co-op. Volunteer, work for free, or help a professor with a project.

Do something work-related. Taking an extra class when you have an opportunity to work is more of the same. It won't meaningfully alter your resume. It rarely will be so insightful that you discover your purpose. When you work, you will get closer to the reality of what comes after you graduate. You will add meaningful experience to your resume. More importantly, it's a great forcing mechanism to help you discover what you like and don't like, and what you are good at vs. what you need to improve on.

Here's an example. I like telling stories using data. I don't like pulling the data from the systems (using SQL, etc.) and I don't need to learn it for the positions I aspire to. I like to pitch and sell my ideas; I don't like to update my boss and others very frequently on our progress in detail (but I have to and need to learn to get good at it). I prefer selling to businesses because I believe I can enhance their operations. I only like selling to consumers if it improves their livelihood and the product is good for them (e.g., I'll never work for a casino). I like having a team and being part of a team. I hate when I have to work at my desk all day. I want my job and my work to be about helping people improve their lives. I'm fairly certain I want to do that via creating services or digital products (vs. physical products). I want to work in an international company, with opportunities to travel and interact with people from many countries.

I've learned the above about myself through experimentation. It's my story, you have your own to discover.

Treat the early part of your adult life and career as such, an experiment to discover yourself. If you are one of the lucky few that already knows what they want with high certainty, we are all envious of you! My Dad loved to paint and draw when he was younger (and was talented at it) which later evolved into a great career in Architecture. He was always certain of his path. For those of us who aren't, experimentation is key.

Benchmarking

This is about figuring out who you are when compared with others. *What is the role you were meant to play?* It's the final key to unlocking your purpose. Let me explain.

You don't control where you are born and who your parents are. You don't control the circumstances in which you have grown up in. In the U.S., we say "those are the cards you were dealt". This is your origin story. If you look at some of the most recognizable people in the world, it's quite frequent that their origin story isn't a great one. They have come from hardships and overcome several obstacles to achieve their goals and purpose. Look up Elon Musk as an example.

Others didn't have hardships growing up but had a unique qualification that affected their self-identity. Jeff Bezos and Steve Jobs were both adopted. You can find these stories everywhere. These circumstances were not chosen, they were dealt to them as a fact of life. As growing children, this led them to experiences and to asking unique questions about life that defined who they are. We all have our own unique origin stories that played a role in defining us. Your story, experiences, questions you asked of life are unique to you. More importantly, they are a clue to discovering what gives you your true energy.

Purpose = True Energy. We talked a lot about what gives you energy, what takes energy away and making lists of those things. The activities that give you energy do so because of who you naturally are (your genes) and because of your origin story (the circumstances you experienced growing up). Experimentation will allow you to better define all the activities that give vs. take your energy. Benchmarking yourself to others will help you see which activities you uniquely excel at.

Each person has strengths in certain areas vs. the others. If you play FIFA or any other video game with characters, they have indicators that define what strengths each character or player excels at. These strengths define what role they play in the team. So far, you have likely compared yourself academically, socially, and physically to others. You are likely good at one of those things (maybe more). But so far in your life, those areas you experienced are narrow compared with what's out there in the world.

As a young adult just starting your career, the world opens up so much opportunity: many different roles, industries, disciplines, people skills, languages, countries to experience, etc. Guess what, you are not trapped anymore! What used to work for you or didn't, doesn't matter now. There is a lot to explore, and as you progress on your adventure, you will discover your strengths, which activities allow you to use those strengths, and which activities you have more energy for.

The activities that allow you to use your strengths, and ones that give you energy, don't necessarily overlap. For example, I like to play FIFA (gives me energy), but I get my ass kicked at the top levels (gaming is not my strength). *When you discover your unique combination of strengths (based on your skills and experience) that also give you energy when you practice them (vs. consume it), you will be on the path to winning.*

In terms of your career, maybe you love creating financial products for entrepreneurs in developing countries. Or you love finding investors for commercial developments. Might be you are interested in developing a service that incentivizes consumers to advertise products on social media. The key here is finding which path you have both strengths AND energy for, not which path you think is interesting or that you might like. Use liking something as a compass, to clue you in to where you might want to experiment, but don't confuse it with where your purpose lies.

Energy matters. *If you can do an activity or pursue a goal or dream longer than anyone else is willing to, you will win.* Even if others are more naturally skilled at a particular topic, if they don't have energy for it, and you do, you will win. When you can find the things that give you energy, they are like your battery, they keep you going. Compare (benchmark) yourself to others to further narrow and understand what roles and activities you excel at.

Dennis Rodman (famous basketball player during the 90s) would average 27 points and 14 rebounds a game when he played competitively in university. He would score, and that's what got him noticed by NBA teams. In an interview many years later he said: "I think the second or third year in the league (NBA), I actually figured out what I can do best – rebound and play defense. I just started learning how to perfect that." That was the role he played with the Chicago Bulls, which led him to fame. Benchmarking himself to other NBA players helped him identify the role he would focus on.

Don't get me wrong, you still have to work hard once you discover your purpose, but by then you will want to work hard for it. You must work on your self-limiting beliefs and fear, and you must develop new skills. You will need to translate your dreams and hopes into goals, because without goals, you are steering a ship with no destination. Your purpose will remain a dream. You have to take action.

Remember that finding your purpose is a journey. Search for paths that contribute positively to society. Experiment to discover your strengths and energy. Benchmark yourself to your peers to validate that those strengths do help you stand out. Look to your past for clues, talk to others who knew you then if it helps. Take your time if you need to. You are more naturally inclined to succeed somewhere, go for it and find where. Believe in yourself and have faith. Good luck!

3. The most important personal gap International Students must address: How you are Perceived

Balancing Perception and Work Quality

When asked, "What is more important, the quality of the work you do or how your work is perceived?", 5 out of 10 international students will say "the quality of work". 9 out of 10 American students recognize that perceived value is more important.

Both answers are not wrong. This is just a clue to how American culture is different. And it's important for you to understand this distinction if you plan on staying in the U.S. and succeeding.

No one will survive and thrive if their work quality is poor. Period. Always aim to improve your work quality throughout your studies and career. However, there is an additional dynamic to consider when you <u>work with others</u> to make projects and initiatives successful. It's easy to demonstrate your work quality with an exam or an essay when you are in charge of the output from beginning to end. What about when you have a group project? Or, when you get your first co-op or internship? Your work quality is now subject to interpretation by others. Since this is not an exam, the answers are not black and white . . . each person's interpretation of your output will be different. Simply doing your best may not translate to a positive interpretation by others.

Don't get me wrong, you likely have some qualities that will stand out, and people will quickly notice them (e.g., if you're smart, friendly, thoughtful, etc.). But the extent of your qualities (e.g., how smart you are in comparison with other internship candidates) is debatable and depends on how others perceive them. My point here is for you to be conscious of this. And ultimately, I advise looking for opportunities to demonstrate your qualities and skills to manage how you are being perceived vs. leaving it to chance.

Many people (including myself) get an allergic reaction at the thought of "showing off" to others. I can see how my advice may sound like I'm suggesting to "showoff". Let's do this simple exercise to better explain my point.

Imagine two students intern at the same company, in identical roles, and with the same boss. If we rated their actual performance vs. how their performance was perceived on a scale of 1 to 10, which student below would stand out to their boss as the better performer?

The Average Joe: (Perceived: 5//Actual: 5)

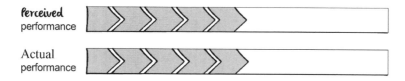

The Idealist: (Perceived: 3//Actual: 7)

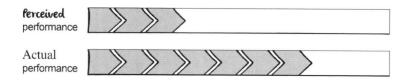

Can you recall people (from high school or university) who seem like the Average Joe and The Idealist?

It's hard to ignore this feels like an unfair situation for the Idealist, who is not getting the full credit they deserve for their work quality and output.

Let's look at another example:

The Schmoozer: (Perceived:8//Actual: 2)

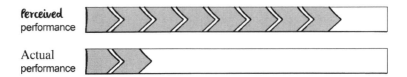

Do you know people like this Schmoozer?

How do they make you feel? . . .

The Idealist is an unfortunate situation that can be remedied by them becoming aware of the importance of managing how they are perceived and taking action to improve it (more on this in later chapters). The problem with the Idealist is they have a bit of an ego about their work, because they are typically good at what they do. They think their work should speak for itself. They feel it should be enough to kick ass every day and do a great job and can't understand why their boss doesn't see what they see. Their boss may even prefer others who are not at the same caliber as them. How they are perceived is a blind spot in their performance they need to prioritize sooner rather than later.

The Schmoozer probably seems like an ass. He or she doesn't care that others may interpret them that way. They understand that perception is important to people, but they over-focus on it and ignore their work quality and actual performance. The Schmoozer will stand out in the short term, but unless they improve their work quality drastically, it's likely the gaps in their performance will come to light soon.

The Average Joe is the mid-long-term winner here. They are perceived as average, but they understand the importance of perception and have demonstrated ability to control how they are perceived. If they improve their work quality, they know how to make others aware of these improvements and will slowly but surely stand out in the long run.

If the above seems unfair, we can all relate. This is the reality of how humans function. We can't control making quick subconscious judgements about others. We rely on interactions with each other to make judgements. It's important to take action to make the most of each interaction now. It matters because 95%+ of jobs out there require you to interact with others, so your success depends on how others perceive you (no more exams to demonstrate your skills). Even if you can succeed in the short term through individual contributions at work (via coding, running your own project where you are the sole contributor, etc.), that will only last so long. As your career progresses, it's inevitable you will have to work with people to succeed. Either way, you will always have a boss and peers, always. They will be judging you, for better or worse. Take action to improve how you are perceived.

Let's look at a final example:

How do you think a CEO fares on their perceived performance vs. actual performance scale?

Remember, he/she is the CEO. The whole company's survival and progress depends on this person.

The Leader: (Perception: 9//Actual: 7)

If the CEO can understand all of the company's functions perfectly, understand the market and all factors affecting their company perfectly, duplicate themselves, and execute on all of these dimensions perfectly, then their actual performance would be very high. That is rarely the case with CEOs. While there are company metrics by which a CEO is measured that make their actual performance less subjective, the point here is they can't execute everything on their own to make those positive metrics happen. Additionally, they are not typically an expert on all the dimensions needed to run a highly effective and successful company. They work with people to make that happen and they represent their company to the public.

Perception is everything here. If they don't inspire investors, the company loses. If they don't inspire customers, they lose. If he or she doesn't inspire their team and all employees, they will definitely lose. You can't inspire all these people by sitting at your desk and focusing on your work. You have to work with people, and you must manage how they perceive you and the direction you are taking to lead them.

The bottom line is, if you are working with people (and you will be all of your career) then you must be mindful of how you are perceived and work on it (especially as many of you have not focused on this in the past). Again, this is not about showing off, this is about knowing you will be judged (mostly subconsciously) and if you don't help people realize what you are worth, they won't magically learn how awesome you are. You have to work on it.

The Communication Skill gap between American and International Students

When was the first time you gave a presentation to a room full of classmates or family? How frequently do you do this? Unfortunately for most international students, the first time is likely in grade six to eight, and the frequency is low (1 or 2 times per year). For many, it may not have been until their first or second year of university. For me, I had presented in a group format in high school, but my first solo presentation was in my second year at university, and it was a disaster. I was called on to give a 1 min talk about any topic I wanted, and I just stood there in front of the class without saying a word. It was embarrassing, I'll never forget it, but it was just the kick in the ass I needed to focus on this skill and improve.

What about a typical American's experience? They present in

school at a very early stage, sometime between first and third grade (something called "show and tell", where they talk about their favorite toy). In Western culture, you are highly encouraged to frequently talk about yourself. International students, however, are highly encouraged to focus on getting good grades. For the last 4 years of K-12, grades are the most important aspect of aspiring international students (note: in most international schools, grades are based more on exam and paper results vs. class participation and presentation). Grades are tangible, and with effort and some skill, they are attainable. You can get good grades all on your own, with hard work. You likely spent the bulk of your time studying, putting your head down and focusing on nailing those exams. This is not true for most students in Western culture, particularly in the U.S. As an example, google "SAT scores by country" and you will notice that China, South Korea, Japan, and Singapore constantly produce better SAT results than the U.S., both with math and reading scores! Watch a couple of American high school movies, and you will notice that being socially popular is prized here. Social skills are encouraged at an early age, and mechanisms are in place to help teach Americans how to showcase their capabilities from childhood. In the last 4 years of high school, in addition to academics, Americans are super focused on extracurricular activities (e.g., school paper, drama club, glee club, band, sports, social impact, etc.). Writing essays is a key part of each of the 4 years, and students often mention the essays they wrote their graduation year in their university applications. These essays and extracurricular activities are highly considered by university admissions teams, besides academics. For Americans, the essays and extracurriculars are how they differentiate themselves from other applicants.

International students typically have to play catch up with their communication skills for the above reasons. Through frequent essay writing and working in groups (via extracurriculars), American students have a solid communication foundation. International students can't afford to ignore this gap and ideally should work to build those skills as soon as their first year at university. Guess what, this is often not what they prioritize. I encourage you to take advantage now that I've slightly made you aware of this gap, and work to improve your communication skills to make your true strengths and work quality be more apparent to others.

International students have great advantages as well. The three qualities that stand out frequently are critical thinking (intelligence), flexibility/adaptability, and courage. You have already ventured on a path that few go on by planning to study and work in the U.S. There are many unknowns, and while you have excitement about all of it, it comes with a lot of fear. The mere fact of putting yourself in this situation suggests you are adaptable and courageous.

In the U.S., going off to college in a different state is a BIG deal. You are going to a different country! Americans go to a different country in their 3rd or 4th year of university, for 4 months (a semester), as part of study abroad programs. For many, this is the first time they travel outside the U.S. You are in a new country, full time, to complete your program, and to potentially stay here for the foreseeable future. That takes guts, so give yourself credit.

In academics, international students typically have worked hard by the time they get accepted to a U.S. university. You have likely completed many external exams (e.g., SATs, APs, Toefl, even British exams like O and A levels). It almost felt like it would never end. You were in a competitive environment, and your school and parents likely highly encouraged you to focus on academics. No wonder we had our heads down and focused on studying. Honestly, in my high school, I rarely had time to do anything besides schoolwork. I remember we had 8 to 10 exams per week, just to help us prepare for the school's final exams. Brutal is the only word to describe it. The result was getting accepted to multiple American universities and making the first two years of my Electrical Engineering degree a breeze.

If you've had to go through something like that, it means you have already spent more time on academics than your average American classmate, which means you are more comfortable with that part of your life. This makes you "appear" to have higher intelligence. You ask a lot of good questions and you dig deep into difficult topics. Give yourself credit for surviving and thriving in your (tough) academic period thus far.

Now, if you can round up your qualities with communication skills, it will make you that much more attractive to a potential employer. The benchmark for communication skills is high, the culture is foreign to you, but with some work, you can quickly improve here. By quickly, I mean if you focus on it and put yourself in environments where you are forced to practice constantly, you will see step change improvements in anywhere between 6 to 12 months. Not enough international students prioritize communication as a skill set, but for you (and me), it may be the most important key to success during a co-op or internship and for your future career (in the U.S. and beyond).

Demonstrating Multiple Skills is a must

When you think more frequently about how you are perceived, it will be important to showcase multiple skills. The more well-rounded you appear, the less risky it will be for someone to hire you, or for your boss to give you an important project. You will come across as more dependable.

Typically, international students are very keen on showing how smart they are or can be. That's their main attempt at showcasing their work and influencing how they are perceived. I see it repeatedly with international co-ops and interns. This is a good thing. You are intelligent and you are leaning on your strengths, which is the right thing to do. I want to offer a perspective that suggests there is a better way and a worse way of showing off your smarts AND that demonstrating just this one skill cannot make you appear dependable (you must demonstrate MULTIPLE skills).

On demonstrating your intelligence to others, when you do it right (with your boss, interviewer, etc.), you will appear intelligent without making the other person feel dumb. The wrong way to do it is to show how smart you are at the expense of the other person feeling less smart (I'm repeating the same sentences twice to help the thought sink in). There are a couple things to think about.

First, there is some level of formal seniority with the people you are interacting with. If they sense that their seniority is being threatened (by demonstrating how they aren't as smart or how they are wrong and you are right) it will affect how they feel about you. Even if they seem above all these frivolous emotions, their perception of you will still be affected in a non-positive way. It's human nature.

Second, don't focus on proving that you are smart by showing you are right. In the real world, intelligence is about knowing that you don't know everything and there may be multiple ways to solve the same problem. Being extremely certain that you are right is ok, but you don't want to demonstrate it in that way. You can challenge someone by asking them questions about their opinions or approach, instead of overtly calling out their approach as faulty. These questions will demonstrate your curiosity and your tact.

Here's an example.

A student co-op once said to me:

"If we run your analysis the way you suggested, it will take too long and it won't be completed in time for the A/B test we want to launch".

ALSO

"Your analysis method does not factor how long it has been since the customer's last order".

They were right. I respected them for calling it out as it avoided errors and delays. Additionally, because they are international students, I didn't mind at all that they gave me those comments as said above (the culture is different, and if you put that aside and focus on the work, they did the right thing). This may not be how others in the U.S. would interpret the student's remarks.

I'm absolutely NOT suggesting that you don't push back when something is wrong. I'm encouraging you to speak up, and you should as frequently as you can in American culture. I'm only suggesting there are ways to do things more tactfully that can get you better results.

Here is a suggestion on how they could have said the same thing to appear smart but not offend anyone:

"I worry that this analysis may take too long. I know it's important to get it done in time for the test, can we discuss additional options to run the analysis?"

ALSO

"I'm thinking if we add how long it's been since the last

customer's order to the analysis, we might get additional useful insights. What do you think?".

Notice, in both new phrases, there is no mention of how something I did was off or wrong. It comes across as more collaborative, open and that we are in this together to make it work. And the student would have appeared to be intelligent for thinking of those things.

Win - Win.

These little details matter and are tough to master.

I want to reiterate a previous point. I'd rather see a student say something vs. not say something. Don't hold back because you are worried about the right way to say it. Say what you need to say, just try to pay more attention to how it makes others feel. Use any feedback you get on your communication to continue to improve your style.

On demonstrating multiple skills, the idea here is not to focus only on intelligence as the skill to demonstrate. Here are other important skills you want to showcase:
• critical thinking
• ability to complete work on time
• flexibility with working on feedback and changing directions with your projects
• ability to make decisions

- communication and persuasion, including the ability to listen well
- team building
- proactiveness
- scrappiness/resourcefulness

These qualities will help you appear more dependable overall. Writing your resume, networking, being in a co-op//internship//full-time job and chatting with your career advisor are all great ways to practice demonstrating the skills mentioned above.

In the upcoming chapters, I will get into detailed examples of how to use each of these opportunities to improve how you are perceived.

4. What to know before starting your job search. Save time by focusing on what works.

Your career journey is exactly that, a journey. It won't be a straight line, there will be twists and turns, there will be ups and downs. If you haven't read Dr. Seuss's book, "Oh, the places you'll go!" I recommend you pick it up. One of the greatest (short) books to read when you are entering a new chapter in life. Books like this, advice like mine, are about equipping you with the tools you need to manage your path to success. All the academic efforts you have spent will pay dividends in your career, but they must be augmented by additional soft skills and a perspective on this next step.

Demystifying the Hiring Process

Before talking about the tools (skills) you need to succeed, I want to paint as clear a picture as possible of what the hiring process, the first hurdle in your journey, looks like.

Many students I speak with have adopted the mindset they need to apply to as many companies as possible. They say, "The more companies I apply to, the higher likelihood I have of getting a job". They are not wrong, it's just that they have increased their chances from 0.0001% to 0.0002%, which isn't enough to justify their effort. Let me explain.

Students typically start by working with a career advisor on their resumes to include all the academic bullets, projects, extracurriculars and//or past work experience. Once the resume is set, they fire it off to as many companies as possible. Many universities have job hub portals where students can see the companies hiring and apply right there. Universities also host companies at career fairs on campus, where students often fumble around for a couple of hours waiting their turn to speak to a recruiter, to drop off their resume, and then leave with no sense of how they can follow up to land a job. And students can apply to most companies in the world via online career portals, LinkedIn pages or Indeed-like websites.

For the application types I mentioned above, if a student applies strictly by submitting their resume, 99.9% won't get an interview. Often, they won't even hear from the company to find out if there has been a decision on their application. This can be extremely frustrating. It's reality.

Here's what's happening.

Once you apply to a company with only a resume, your resume gets collected in a pile with every other applicant's resume and tagged to the type of role you are applying for. At this stage, companies have a singular goal of collecting as many resumes as possible!

This increases the odds of them filling that role within a set deadline. Can you imagine how many applicants apply to Amazon, Google or Microsoft? It's staggering to think about.

Next, the company must filter applicants to those who they believe have a good chance of passing the first interview. I've chosen my words carefully. The company looks for candidates who they believe can pass a phone interview (typically the next step in the hiring process), not necessarily ones with the best profile that matches the job description (although that is typically a good indicator of a candidate who would pass the phone interview, it's not always the case that they are selected). Your resume is subject to biases such as nationality, age, sex, written English quality, etc. This is not fair, but it's reality, and the more we understand how things work, the better we can make them work for us.

In small or mid-sized companies that don't employ software to screen applicants' resumes, recruiters from their Talent//HR team manually screen as many resumes as they can.

This is a super time-consuming process. What happens is recruiters spend very little time reading each resume, typically an average of 6 seconds. Additionally, it's unlikely that they will see every applicant's resume by the time they fill a role.

So, the odds for your resume are that they either get reviewed for 6 seconds, or they don't get read at all. When a resume does get read, recruiters lean on their sense of the type of candidate that would pass the next step (typically phone interview), and additionally consider how the employees that will be conducting these phone interviews might judge this resume (since those employees decide to keep you in the interview process after the phone screen). The recruiter uses their best judgement in those 6 seconds, trying to ignore any biases they have, and then pass or not pass a candidate. There is fatigue involved as well. After reading 20 resumes in a row, the recruiter will get tired and lean more and more on their biases (which may or may not favor you). They may spend even less time on average per resume. It's possible, I have seen it happen.

Larger or more sophisticated companies use algorithms to screen resumes.

They look for specific keywords and patterns in the documents to decide whether to move forward with an application. It's difficult to find out how any company's algorithm chops up and consumes a resume (if you find out, or create software to find out, let me know, could be a great idea for a startup). Either way, spending time to figure it out just gets you past the first stage, so it's not worth the effort.

The bottom line is, submitting your resume is not enough. You must be selective about where you want to apply and build up your networking skills to better navigate each company's application process. More on that later.

If you get selected for an initial phone interview, congrats! This means that the recruiter believes you will pass the phone interview, so pat yourself on the back. You have to prepare well for this step (will talk about that in the next chapter), but what's critical now is for you to learn more about the person you will be speaking with. If it's someone from the recruiting team, then this call is an additional screen to make sure you are a fit.

The recruiter will want to listen to you speak and get a sense of how you conduct yourself in a conversation.

If you do well, they will schedule a follow-up call with an employee or hiring manager from one of the departments with open positions (those individuals make final decisions on you as an applicant). The recruiter's level of knowledge about the roles they are responsible for filling varies. There is a possibility that they don't know a lot about the role you are applying to and may not be able to perfectly answer your detailed questions about what the role entails. It's important for you to consider that. They are more interested in hearing you talk about your background to see if a hiring manager would be interested in your profile. They want to gauge if you would work well with others in the company (aka if you are a fit with their company's culture). So, many biases and judgements play a role during the call.

A great goal for students is to focus on building rapport with the recruiter. If you can show you are friendly, can get along with others, and that your background is the same as the person in your resume (that you are who you say you are), you will pass this phone screen.

The final part of the hiring process is to get you (the applicant) in front of employees and hiring managers who you might work with or report to. This could be additional calls, but ultimately concludes with onsite interviews. Note: for co-ops or internships, final decisions are typically made after phone interviews. Full-time roles require an onsite visit. We will talk more about interviews and how to make your best self stand-out.

To summarize, if you are an international student just starting to apply by filling applications and sending your resume, the hiring process looks like this:

You drop your resume at the top, cross your fingers, and hope you get asked for the initial phone screen. There is less than a 1% chance of you getting a phone call.

You need a better way to get hired.

But there isn't a magic bullet. You will have to work for it.

It starts with focusing on building life-long career skills, specifically, with **writing and networking**. These skills will be key for writing enticing cover letters, tailored resumes, establishing contact with recruiters and gaining inside knowledge of a company's organizational structure or pain points . . . all key to help get your application to the next stage.

A note on work authorization: Many companies ask in their applications if you have authorization to work in the U.S. Work with your university and do some research online to determine if you do, and then answer the question truthfully (you don't want to go down a path that's a dead-end, and waste your time). And there are resources like myvisajobs.com that show which companies have hired students with your visa status in the past. Filtering down your job search to those companies will save you a ton of headache down the road. Navigating your job search with this additional visa hurdle isn't easy and is an extra challenge the international student faces. There is a ton of value in networking with the companies you are interested in, regardless of whether they sponsor international students, because it's a great learning opportunity and you never know who you might meet in the process that can help you land a job somewhere. Just be truthful whenever that question comes up. If you are really keen on a company, work with your university's visa advisor to come up with creative ways to pitch the employer on applying for a visa for you (easier said than done, but it's been done).

Pay Attention in your Writing Classes

Very few students think writing is an important skill to develop. You've probably taken a writing class in the past. Where did it rank in your list of priorities? I bet it wasn't high on that list.

Outside of your writing classes, university application essay (which you probably got help with) and resume, you had little need to focus on writing as a skill. Writing is very underrated, and is timeless for your career, both for searching for a job and for succeeding in your job, particularly in the U.S.

Like many international students, I didn't focus on my English classes, essay classes or even the technical writing classes during my engineering degree. I focused on core classes like C++, Statistics, Applied Math, etc. I saw these writing classes as a means to an end (I just need to pass and get them over with), and my parents did too (so they never pressured me to focus here). They were right. For that particular point of time, my grades in core classes mattered more to progress and to get accepted to a good university. But to find a job, what you need becomes very different. You need to network, and you need to present yourself well on paper and in person. It's all about how you are perceived, and first impressions are important (they are hard to change once someone has made up their mind about you).

First impressions are usually developed in the first 90 seconds of meeting someone. However, most of the networking and first impression opportunities during your job search will not be in person. They will be via your resume, cover letter, LinkedIn messages and emails and you want to put your best foot forward in each. Your career advisor, even your mentor (if you have one), can't possibly help you review each instance of your writing. You have no choice but to write for yourself. So, when you are seriously considering applying for an internship, co-op, or full-time role, take this as an opportunity to really hone your writing skills.

Meet with your career advisor and learn from their feedback. Many students just want to spend time with an advisor to get their resume written, so they can start applying. Don't be that person. Spend time, ask questions, understand the resume writing framework, and then write your resume knowing you will need to do this over and over again (now, and later in your career). When you network, a lot of contacts you will be interested in connecting with will be alumni (whom your university has advised you to connect with) and people who work in companies you are interested in. The initial communication you send them will likely be via email or LinkedIn (I will show many examples, good and bad, in the Networking chapter). What should you say? How should you say it? How should you write it? Will the person you are reaching out to understand what you meant when they read what you wrote, or will it get lost in translation? Your writing must be good, so your point is clear. This is especially true in the U.S., where extreme clarity in communication and the meaning you are trying to convey is the norm. Now is a good time to get good at this skill and searching for a job is a great way to practice.

When you start working, your writing skills will make or break you. You must write well-structured performance reviews, emails to your clients, or to your boss's boss. You must pitch an idea on paper, internally or if you work for a startup, to investors. There is no escaping writing, it's a key part of communication.

For me, the first time it hit me that I was not confident about my writing skills but needed to be, was way too late in my career (I wish I was advised to focus on it earlier). I had already been working in the U.S. for 8 years and was preparing my application to INSEAD for a full-time MBA. I had to write ten essays! I also needed to prepare a resume in INSEAD's format (I hadn't updated my resume in a very long time at that point). The stakes were high for me. I really wanted a change, and in all my attempts prior to applying for an MBA, the only options I could find was to move to a different company but in a similar role and industry. When I searched for roles I thought I wanted, at companies that attracted me, it was clear they would not accept me without relevant past experience OR an MBA. So, I focused on the MBA. I wanted to get into a good school to increase my chances of changing the industry I worked in, to one I was more excited about. But ten essays, a resume and a great GMAT score were in my way. I was overwhelmed. And GMAT was the least of my worries. I ended up finding a consultant I liked to coach me through the application process and help me write . . . and spent $4,000 USD for their service! I convinced myself, this would increase my chances of getting accepted, and at the least, would improve my writing skills (which I finally realized were important).

I got accepted, and during my MBA, I applied to and was hired for a role and company that were just right for me. What I didn't realize then, was that MBA roles are all about communication. You are managing people, managing projects, managing external partners and clients.

I had good experience managing people and external clients (mostly via oral communication), but my written skills were extremely poor (by the standards expected of an MBA graduate). I had to highlight my team's progress in a monthly report and present it to the leadership team. I had to organize a strategy document for the vertical I managed, and gain alignment on the plan. My challenge wasn't a lack of ideas or plan, it was to get it on paper in a way that can be consumed easily and captures all the key points. But I kept thinking that all the points were important! How was I supposed to condense all this material to a more easily consumable format? I didn't want to leave out details that made the plan make sense. While this is true, my boss and boss's boss don't have all the time in the world to read my plan. I need to be able to present something concise.

Ever heard of an elevator pitch? An elevator pitch is based on the premise that if you had 60-90 secs to pitch an idea to someone important, that you happen to bump into in an elevator, what would you say? I had to have an elevator pitch for my plan as well as a 5 min pitch, a 5 min read document, a 1-page summary, a deep dive document, etc.

I struggled to say the least. But I am 10X more effective at my job now than I ever was in the past. I can get my ideas across to others, regardless of who they are, and what circumstance I am under to present. I am forever grateful at the opportunity to focus on honing this skill. It's worth noting that leaders in Engineering, Data Science and Marketing are in the same boat and have to lean on this skill to move their agendas forward.

A Data Science Director with strong communication skills is often significantly more effective at their job than a Director with the same technical skill set but lacks communication strengths. It doesn't matter what field you are in, as you progress into management positions, your job will become more about communication than anything else. You will lean on your team to figure out the details, you will guide them, and you will make sure the rest of the company feels good about your team's path forward.

Here's one more nod to writing and communication in general.

Legendary investor and billionaire Warren Buffet had a tip for young people recorded on a video posted to LinkedIn. He said, "The one easy way to become worth 50 percent more than you are now - at least - is to hone your communication skills - both written and verbal. If you can't communicate, it's like winking at a girl in the dark - nothing happens. You can have all the brainpower in the world, but you have to be able to transmit it. And the transmission is communication."

Why Networking matters

Networking is about developing a connection with others. Connection is developed through "likeness", meaning by finding similarities between you and the person you are attempting to connect with.

Every student at every university studying any degree is encouraged to network. It's such a buzz word. And it's often tied with a feeling of yuck! Very few students tell me they look forward to networking events. The common feeling it musters up is a feeling of "I'm being fake" and "I'm being manipulative". Students know they need to network to find a job. In that process, their position is one of wanting something from someone else, and that someone else is a stranger. They think, why would that stranger ever want to help? Students often hear advice and tips like smile, be friendly, ask questions, etc. . . . but that doesn't answer the question of how to deal with a situation where you want something from someone. Yes, you should smile and be friendly when you meet new people, that is a given . . . the point often left out of generic advice is that networking is about ***developing a connection, NOT about asking for a job***. I will repeat this several times throughout the book. Connect with others first, don't ever ask for a job first.

Well then, why should I network if I can't ask for a job? You can, and you should, but in due time. You must establish a connection first. There are things you can ask of strangers and things you can't. You can ask a random person for a piece of gum or mint . . . you can't ask them for $100. Or even $5. You can ask your close friend for $10 to get lunch because you forgot your wallet, or even $100 if you absolutely needed it.

Asking a stranger at a networking event, via email or LinkedIn for a job is like asking them for $100. You are just not at that point in the relationship yet. It's no different than taking the SAT exam. You can take it with no prep, you might get lucky and do well. Odds are, you won't. If you warm up to the SAT, via practice questions, timing yourself on a whole sample test, working on areas that can be challenging, then you can expect a better result. Meeting people is no different. You have to work your way to a better spot with them, and we will talk about how to do that in the networking chapter.

It's worth noting now that you cannot establish good rapport with everyone. You will jive with some people, you won't with others. That's ok. What matters is that you don't get discouraged and that you keep searching for the folks you jive with.

Once you get good at meeting others and developing quick rapport, the whole world opens up to you. The difference in your life becomes incredible. This is a tool you can use anywhere, whether you are at an airport, at school, hiking or even at a restaurant. Knowing you have this tool in your toolbox and can pull it out whenever you need to, is a great feeling. More importantly, you will use it to open doors for yourself in your professional career.

When searching for a job, networking is key to unlocking opportunities. The strategy here is to be more targeted with your approach by selecting a handful of companies to really focus on. Work with your career advisor and browse company websites to figure out what kind or roles and industries you are interested in, and leverage university resources and websites to narrow down to companies that have sponsored students (from your field) in the past. Once you have selected your targets, you should do in-depth research on each. Read about open roles and search LinkedIn for people that already have those roles at those companies. These folks are a great way to learn more about the roles, to find out more in-depth information about the company, AND to potentially have them advocate for you at those companies and offer to refer you for a job. Companies typically have a process by which current employees can refer external candidates to open roles.

But how can you get those people to become advocates for you? Through informational interviews, small talk, and a ton of practice to find your style that works well with people.

Once you have your target companies in mind, it becomes like solving a puzzle. You have to find the pieces (read about the roles, find people in those roles) and then use networking to put the pieces together (talk to those people, learn more about the company, find someone you jive with who would be an advocate for you).

I wish I was advised early on to follow this process. I would have had a tremendous head start in my career and not feared moving to new companies (most people don't change jobs out of fear of the process of finding a new one).

To network successfully, you have to practice. You will fail, repeatedly, but that will be ok, because you have adopted a growth mindset and understand this is part of the process of you becoming who you want to be. When you succeed, it will feel like you climbed and conquered a mountain. Especially with the first win you get out of networking (which could be the first time a person who once was a stranger refers you to a job). You will say to yourself, "Damn! That was hard. I'm not sure I can put that much effort each time with every new person". I'll tell you that the second and third win might be just as hard, if not harder. But once you get good, you can succeed more frequently and with less effort. This tool (your networking skills) becomes lighter in your hands, and you can use it at will. Practice, practice, practice, have faith, and then watch how you will succeed.

5. The standard path to finding a job: How to excel with each step

If you are an undergrad, start your job search as early as your 2nd or 3rd semester. If you are a graduate student or PHD, start right away.

Despite my many attempts to convince students to start early, they typically start their job search 3 months before they graduate (I wasn't much better when I was an undergrad). You are putting way too much pressure on yourself if you wait till then.

A five to ten-year experienced professional can take three to six months on average to find a new role, and that is if they did nothing else but focus on finding a job. If job hunting is new to you, there are many building blocks and personal growth steps you need to face before you see results. Take my advice, start soon.

At university, you will have more than a few resources to support your job search. Take advantage of each, they are part of why your tuition fees are so high.

My advice below attempts to help you focus only on the things that matter the most with job hunting. In an era where you have a ton of resources and information, it's easy to get overwhelmed. What I've found helpful for me at the start of any journey is to focus on one or two things, and keep them in the back of my mind as I progress. I've boiled down the most important aspects to focus on for each of these job-hunting levers:

• Working with your Career Advisor

• Writing work experience bullets in your Resume

• Achieving great outcomes from Career Fairs

• Understanding Interview dynamics

Take Advantage of Having a Career Advisor

Career services departments at universities work hard to create and maintain high-quality services for their students. Some universities do it better than others. Some even consider international students' unique challenges and organize different events and programs to help their search (e.g., bringing in immigration lawyers to advise on the latest regulations, or international students who have graduated and successfully found a full-time role in the U.S., to share their experience). As an example, when I can make time, I visit universities in the Boston area to share material from this book with international students. Career services departments are there to support you, but they are not there to do the work for you.

There are a ton of free resources from career services departments, including reading/listening/video material, alumni databases, networking events, panel discussions, etc. Make yourself aware of your school's resources and events. Be proactive, don't wait for them to contact you, they may not.

Career counselors, employees of career services departments, typically offer as much support as possible to make students' job searches successful. Some of the services include:

- Resume and cover letter help
- Mock interviews
- Review LinkedIn profile content
- Consult on job search strategy
- Answer career search questions
- Coach you on how to network
- Brainstorm ideas with you
- and more . . .

Remember though, that they are not the final answer to your finding a job. They will give you an assessment based on what you want and need to do, and give you different avenues to explore, but you need to ultimately choose what path you go down and do the work. They will not hold your hand through your journey.

For example, career services can set up networking events with employers, bring in people to teach networking, and coach you 1:1 on your approach. What they won't do is give you their contacts from different employers or introduce you. A lot of international students expect that career services just hand over specific employer contacts for students to reach out to for a job. Think about it, a university's employer contacts are ones that they have developed over many years. They will not hand them over to students and risk screwing up those relationships. They WILL set up networking events, encourage employers to hire interns and co-ops from their school, but they WON'T give the students their employer contacts.

I won't lie, I expected to get employer contacts as well when I was an undergrad. Our whole life, the academic part has been very structured, so we expect this part to be the same. Finding a job is not that straightforward, unfortunately, and career services can help but not all the way. You own your success here. This is the part that is very American vs. other cultures (although schools outside the U.S. don't do the hand holding either). It's just that in the U.S., Americans are raised with that independence, so international students come across as expecting too much from career services. You have to be more independent with your job search and use career services to support you (not hand hold you through it).

Career counselors often recall the same themes with things that international students could do better with their job search. They say students often come to them at the last minute (close to graduation) for help with networking or their resume. They will help, but it will take a miracle at that point for you to find a job by the time you graduate. They point out that international students will often ask career counselors to help write or rewrite their resumes. Career counselors are not the grammar or spelling police. They will not go line by line through your resume. They will help you with a bullet or two, so you get the idea on how to write bullets the correct way, then it's on you to wrap it up.

Students also come with a long laundry list of all the questions they have related to job search. While the counselor typically appreciates that students are prepared for the meeting, if the questions are super random and don't help the student with a particular part of their search, it does not feel like a valuable use of time for both parties. The better approach here is to come with a list of 10 (at most) of your most important questions, around a single theme (e.g., how to select companies and roles to apply to) for a more productive conversation.

International students specifically lean a lot on what their friends or peers are doing with their job searches. If they hear a career advisor advise something that is contrary to what they heard from friends, it's difficult for the student to reconcile the two opposing points of view. There's some FOMO (fear of missing out) going on. For example, if all of a student's peers are putting a summary section in their resume, or putting "searching for a co-op" in their LinkedIn title . . . then they should be doing that as well (even if the career counselor advises against it). The right approach here is to get as much feedback from others to help you make a more informed decision. To do that, you need to internalize the feedback. What career counselors often see is students zig-zagging from one strategy to another with their job search. They take the advice du jour and apply it without necessarily thinking if it will work for them. I don't blame them. Students don't know or have much experience with this topic yet. They are experimenting, and they are doing it under the pressure of finding a job, hoping the companies sponsor them and that their visas get approved. It's tough. These themes result from students starting their job search late and then panicking.

Here are the things that some students have done that make them stand out to career counselors. FYI, you don't need to stand out to the career counselor, but it's an advantage if you do. Think of it as practicing your networking skills. The better relationship you can develop with a career counselor, the more they will root for you, support you, and potentially advocate for you. A great tip to start a conversation for the first time with a career counselor is to ask them what services they offer, and what's the best way you (the student) can engage with them. You'll get bonus points.

More advanced students come for support with "how to brand themselves". They seek advice on their LinkedIn profile, their posts, and the language they are using to contact people to network. They also seek counseling on how to select an industry/company/role they want before they apply. They discuss what they like and their motivations (e.g., are they in this major because their parents pushed them, or because money is a big motivator or both). They want the counselor to play devil's advocate with their approach and their thinking, leveraging them as a sounding board to their ideas. They ask for support with double checking their emails, resume, cover letter vs. asking them "how to write them from scratch". They show some of that independence upfront. Counselors love that. No counselor wants to work on resumes with students all day (but that's, unfortunately, a bulk of the interaction they have with students). They want to work on the meaty, real stuff like how they can help you with bigger things such as key decisions you are making or your job search strategy.

I heard this great example of how a student helped a counselor by organizing an event to have a supply ops professional give a talk on campus. The student offered the idea, was proactive in reaching out to their contacts from their past co-op and helped organize the session. Since then, the counselor has advocated for the student when they needed a reference. Bottom line is, treat your career counselor as someone you are trying to network with. Look for their advice, not for them to do the work for you. Pre-plan your meetings with them and do as much work as you can in advance to make the most of your time with them. And if the opportunity arises, look for ways to support them (it doesn't hurt to ask them how you can help).

Write Great Work Experience Bullets for your Resume

There are plenty of free resources (online at your school) that provide templates and advice on how to write your resume. Don't forget to leverage your career advisor for one on one support as well. In this part of the chapter, I want to share my personal method for writing one part of the resume: the Work Experience bullets.

As I mentioned before, when looking for a job, past work experience is more highly regarded than additional academic courses you've completed.

The courses you signed up for are a signal of where your interests lie, more than anything else. Not all academic courses are created equal. Some courses will allow you to list practical skills such as foreign languages, SQL, or Python, and are more valuable on your resume than other theory-based courses. They signal you are trying to get ahead of having to learn these skills on the job. Again, this is my opinion, one data point, take it with a grain of salt.

Recruiters will gravitate towards your major, GPA and your past work experience in the 6 seconds allocated to read your resume. Your GPA indicates that you met the minimum qualifications to work at their company, and if it's very strong, it will tick off a green flag in the recruiter's mind (you get bonus points). If it's the minimum requirement or below, red flag (everything else on your resume better be spectacular). They will assess if you can work with people, thereby looking for anything in your resume that signals leadership and team working skills (intelligence and critical thinking qualities are typically inferred by your GPA). The two places the recruiter will gravitate to are past work experience and extracurricular activities or interests you've highlighted.

Early in my career, when I started writing resumes, I couldn't for the life of me understand why I had to include "interests" and "extracurricular activities". I had the attitude that my schoolwork should speak for itself and be enough . . . check out my GPA, my classes and projects, they are rock solid, I thought. Just because I attended classes, and was forced to complete projects to graduate, does not indicate to the recruiter my ability to work with people. I didn't know at the time that this is what they were filtering for. With school projects, I knew many students back in the day who barely participated or contributed their share, and rode on the shoulders of others to pass those classes. Sometimes, when I didn't have enough time, I was one of those students. So were the recruiters. They know what's up and recognize that your classes and projects are not indicative of your group working skills.

Again, if you have time over the summer or during a semester to do additional work, try to join a group (something extracurricular) or find an internship or summer job. This will be a better use of time and will create more opportunities to highlight your ability to work with others.

The goal from your work experience (or extracurricular activities) bullets are to:

• Demonstrate additional skills that complement your intelligence qualities, particularly people skills

• Highlight that you understood the value you brought in your role

• Do the above in a concise way (so that it can be consumed in 4-6 secs)

Here's the framework for writing these bullets:

1. Write down as many details, in chronological order, as you can remember from your work experience. Don't forget to jot down your people interaction details.

2. Determine the skills demonstrated through this experience

3. Summarize your content into concise bullets, showcasing:

    a. Why this project or task was important (what value did it bring to the company)?

    b. What did you do (what skills were demonstrated)?

    c. What were the results?

4. Leverage your career advisor to get feedback

I've provided an example below, from one of my co-op's experiences, to show you how to do this right.

Co-op Resume - Work Bullets Example

1. Write down as many details, in chronological order, as you can remember from your work experience. Don't forget to jot down your people interaction details.

I was assigned a customer segmentation project from the category team. The goal was to dig into multiple inputs of customer data using SQL, and then to group the customers into segments to gain insights. We wanted insights to grow sales, as we suspected that many of our customers were not returning to shop with us. I didn't know SQL, and had to learn it from scratch. I had little analytics experience. I found a course on my employers' learning hub and signed up for it. I practiced simple queries, and quickly learned that google and YouTube were great with answering the many challenges I faced. The tough part was learning my employers' database, specifically where the different data lived. This is where I got some support from Mike (pricing team), who helped me as I struggled. Additionally, Lauren (from my team) was helpful when I couldn't get a query to work. I had to work with my boss to get a list of the different customer data points to start with. Sometimes, I suggested (successfully) adding data points for us to consider in the analysis. Example: added data on when the customer placed their first order ever on our site. Brian (from my team) had some experience with a similar exercise. Once I had an initial set of data, I reviewed it with him to see if he thought I was missing anything, and to get ideas on what the insights might be.

As I've been working on this project, I've frequently updated my boss on progress//issues, but I wanted an opportunity to highlight my being proactive with the insights, showing I took the initiative to think of additional ideas (this is where Brian helped). I made a couple of edits and shared the final customer data output with my boss. We determined that 80% of our revenue came from 20% of our customers. We also saw that the high spending 20% bought categories of product that the rest (the 80%) didn't. Since these customers are businesses, our next step was to learn more profile details about who our top spenders are (what sub-category of business they are, what services they provide, where they are in the country and how many employees they have).

The goal was to find customers in the 80% with a similar profile to our top customers (the 20% top spenders) and run a campaign targeting them with the categories they haven't shopped from us yet. Our theory was that they probably didn't know that we carry these categories, so we wanted to make them aware and give them an incentive (small discount) to buy them.

2. Determine the skills demonstrated through your experience

Here is the list of skills you want to demonstrate. Feel free to find additional ones online; these are the basics:

• critical thinking

• ability to complete work on time

• flexibility in working with feedback and being able to pivot or change direction with your projects

• ability to make decisions

• communication and persuasion

• team building/collaboration

• proactiveness

• scrappiness/resourcefulness

Remember the skills you demonstrate result from the actions you took on the job, not the "why the project was of value" or "what the result is". You will need to include those as well, and they will help demonstrate your critical thinking (but not other skills). And talking about the why and result is the norm now, so if you don't, it's a clear sign to the recruiter you didn't prepare the resume well.

What was demonstrated from the example?

-- Critical Thinking -- Scrappiness/Resourcefulness

I didn't know SQL, and had to learn it from scratch. I also had little analytics experience. I found a course on my employers' learning hub and signed up for it. I practiced simple queries, and quickly learned that google and YouTube were great with answering the many challenges I faced.

Commentary: Not everyone can learn SQL from scratch or has the confidence to try. This demonstrates that the co-ops intelligence and past school experience has prepared them for this challenge (critical thinking). Their initiative to find resources to help them learn speaks of their independence (scrappiness/resourcefulness). It says that the co-op is ok with everything not being perfectly organized and handed to them in a perfectly tidy package (e.g., the company should have a rigorous training program to help them learn, but it didn't, and that didn't bother the co-op).

-- Communication and Persuasion -- Team Building/Collaboration

The tough part was learning my employers' database, specifically where the different data lived. This is where I got some support from Mike (pricing team), who helped me as I struggled. Additionally, Lauren (from my team) was helpful when I couldn't get a query to work.

Commentary: When you can demonstrate that you worked with people to get the thing you need to do your job well, nothing is more powerful (assuming you did it in a collaborative and friendly way). Our co-op faced a challenge and had to figure out who could help. They had to somehow muster up the courage to ask that person for help (if you are stuck, you should always ask for help, always) and worked with them to get the knowledge they needed (communication and persuasion). It seems the co-op was able to go back to these individuals multiple times, meaning they built some sort of rapport, which is the beginning part of building better working relationships with their peers (team building).

-- Critical Thinking -- Flexibility -- Ability to make decisions -- Communication and Persuasion -- Team Building/Collaboration -- Proactiveness

I had to work with my boss to get a list of the different customer data points to start with. Sometimes, I suggested (successfully) adding data points for us to consider in the analysis. Example: added data on when the customer placed their first order ever on our site. Brian (from my team) had some experience with a similar exercise. Once I had an initial set of data, I reviewed it with him to see if he thought I was missing anything, and to get ideas on what the insights might be. As I've been working on this project, I've frequently updated my boss on progress//issues, but I wanted an opportunity to highlight my being proactive with the insights, showing I took the initiative to think of additional ideas (this is where Brian helped). I made a couple of edits and shared the final customer data output with my boss

Commentary: This note is my favorite as it demonstrates a wide variety of skills. Can you feel it? This person sounds like they are someone you can depend on. They are thinking independently, speaking up, working with others to solve problems. Overall a great combo. The co-op suggested to their boss to add more data, signaling they understand the larger goal of this project (to get insights) and that they are thinking independently about how to solve the problem (critical thinking, ability to make decisions). That this suggestion was accepted says that the student had a good hunch, but more than that it suggests an ability to convince their boss on their ideas (communication and persuasion). Their idea of sourcing someone else's thoughts on this problem is brilliant, especially since that other person has worked on a similar project (proactiveness, flexibility, team building). This helps make the co-op's project output even more convincing, since others have viewed it (which increases the chances that the insights are in the right direction). This shows they are being very thoughtful about the approach.

3. Summarize into concise bullets

a. Why this project or task was important (what value did it bring to the company):

You must demonstrate (via your resume) that you understood the problem you were working on. Initially in your career, you will be heavily focused on tactical execution work. You will get good reviews if you can perform your work well and collaborate with others successfully. You will stand out and get excellent reviews if you can demonstrate that you understand the overarching goal of what you, your boss, and even your boss's boss, are trying to accomplish. When you become a leader in the company, you will define the problems to be solved to grow the business, and you will have teams to help you solve them. Think about the overarching problems the company is trying to solve, how your work fits in, and even suggest ideas to get a head start. Highlight in your resume that you have thought this way, even if just through a co-op or internship, to make the right impression. More and more students are doing this, so it's becoming the norm. Make sure you are doing it as well.

Going back to our example:

I was assigned a customer segmentation project from the category team. The goal was to dig into multiple inputs of customer data using SQL, and then to group the customers into segments to gain insights. We wanted insights to grow sales, as we suspected that many of our customers were not returning to shop with us.

This becomes . . .

• Led customer segmentation project; generated insights to recommend next steps to get customers to buy from "COMPANY NAME" more frequently

Even more concise . . .

• Led customer segmentation project; generated insights to boost customer repeat purchases

I used the word "Led" because the student was the main organizer and executor of this project. No, they were not the boss, but this project's success rested on their shoulders, so they "Led" it. This is a good keyword that all students should use in their resumes. The problem they were working on was that customers were not coming back to buy again (repeat purchases were low) and the goal of the project was to recommend ideas (based on insights) to get them to come back and purchase. The bulk of the work the student did was "generate insights", which is why you can summarize a lot of the work to those two simple words. Remember, the more concise, the better (the more likely that it will be read).

b. What was it that you did (what skills were demonstrated):

Here you want to talk about what you did, demonstrate as many skills as possible, and specifically emphasize your people skills.

I didn't know SQL, and had to learn it from scratch. I had little analytics experience. I found a course on my employers' learning hub and signed up for it. I practiced simple queries, and quickly learned that google and YouTube were great with answering the many challenges I faced. The tough part was learning my employers' database, specifically where the different data lived. This is where I got some support from Mike (pricing team), who helped me as I struggled. Additionally, Lauren (from my team) was helpful when I couldn't get a query to work. I had to work with my boss to get a list of the different customer data points to start with. Sometimes, I suggested (successfully) adding data points for us to consider in the analysis. Example: added data on when the customer placed their first order ever on our site. Brian (from my team) had some experience with a similar exercise.

Once I had an initial set of data, I reviewed it with him to see if he thought I was missing anything, and to get ideas on what the insights might be. As I've been working on this project, I've frequently updated my boss on progress/issues, but I wanted an opportunity to highlight my being proactive with the insights, showing I took the initiative to think of additional ideas (this is where Brian helped). I made a couple of edits and shared the final customer data output with my boss.

Skills demonstrated: -- *Critical Thinking* -- *Flexibility* -- *Ability to make decisions* -- *Communication and Persuasion* -- *Team Building/Collaboration* -- *Proactiveness* -- *Scrappiness/Resourcefulness*

Becomes . . .

• Analyzed customer data from SQL (self-trained during co-op); successfully recommended and sourced several ideas on analysis method and collaborated with the pricing and category teams on the final output

Even more concise . . .

• Analyzed customer data (using SQL, self-trained); recommended analysis method ideas, collaborated with the pricing/category teams

I know that this feels like it does not capture the whole story. That's OK! That's not the goal here. Save the whole story for the interview. The point here is to demonstrate as many skills as possible in as concise a way as possible. You have to reduce the story to its simplest form. Think of it as "what keywords capture my story with this project, and do they demonstrate a broad amount of skills".

Keywords like "Analyzed" and "Self-trained" showcase critical thinking and scrappiness/resourcefulness. "Recommended" showcases communi-cation and persuasion, and ability to make decisions. "Collaborated" suggests team building. What's missing here in terms of skills demonstrated but haven't come through in the bullets are Flexibility and Proactiveness. It's OK if you can't fit them all in. We already captured 5 skills in a simple bullet . . . save the rest of the story for the interview.

If you still feel the above is a bit dry . . .

• Analyzed customer data (using SQL, self-trained); recommended including additional data sets to gain better insights (e.g., date of customer's first purchase, categories purchased, time since last order, etc.) and collaborated with the pricing/category teams on the final output

Here we didn't showcase additional skills, rather added more color to what was done and how the co-op thought about the problem. We also made the bullet a lot longer. If you only have one such work experience project to highlight in your resume, use the long form. If you have a lot of experience you want to capture (from multiple jobs or extracurricular activities), use the super concise form. The most important part you can't skip, whether your bullet is longer or more concise, is to make sure multiple skills are highlighted.

So far, we have one bullet on "Why this was valuable" and one on "What we did". Let's wrap this up with the "Results".

c. What were the results:

Employers recognize that a lot of skills that their employees need will be acquired or learned on the job, not at school. Typical classes at university will not perfectly prepare you for real-life work. This is particularly true for entry-level jobs (first job after an undergraduate degree). So, that you did this activity or that activity on a job is only somewhat relevant. What's more important is what you learned, and why that would be valuable to a new employer's open role.

The employer often needs to dig much deeper to extract what you learned from a past job. Highlighting the why, the skills demonstrated, the <u>tangible results</u> on your resume is key, and will help the employer get the gist of what you learned (they will dig deeper during the interview). I see a lot of entry-level resume bullets saying something like "Analyzed data set to predict accident severity". Done. Or "Wrote complex SQL queries for big data manipulation. Improved user interface experience". These aren't bad, but they are not great. The last example tried to showcase a result, "Improved user experience", but that's an intangible outcome. How was it improved? Which part? What metric suggests that it was improved? Also, because you are diligent readers and read the previous two sections without falling asleep (wink, wink), you noticed those two examples don't highlight multiple skills. Working on some analytics project potentially highlights some critical thinking skills, nothing more.

We determined that 80% of our revenue came from 20% of our customers. We also saw that the high spending 20% bought categories of product that the rest (the 80%) didn't. Since these customers are businesses, our next step was to learn more profile details about who our top spenders are (what sub-category of business they are, what services they provide, where they are in the country and how many employees they have). The goal was to find customers in the 80% with a similar profile to our top customers (the 20% top spenders) and run a campaign targeting them with the categories they haven't shopped from us yet. Our theory was that they probably didn't know that we carry these categories, so we wanted to make them aware and give them an incentive (small discount) to buy them.

Becomes . . .

• Determined that shopping habits of top 20% of customers differ significantly from the rest; identified high potential customer profiles (from bottom 80%) and aligned on a product category "awareness" campaign to target them

Even more concise . . .

• Identified high potential customers not yet purchasing frequently; aligned on a marketing campaign to target them

Both examples work. It just depends on how much you want to emphasize this work experience vs. other work experience on your resume. On Keywords, did you notice the word "aligned"? We could have easily written the word "planned". "Aligned" suggests you worked with others to get this done. "Organized" can also portray that same idea, which is to showcase you have experience working in a team environment.

4. Leverage your career advisor to provide you feedback

Use your career advisor as a sounding board. Get feedback on the bullets you created, ask them to coach you through a couple grammar or spelling issues. Take with you the long form note you wrote (from step 1). It will come in handy if your advisor feels the bullets are too narrow, or if they want to highlight something they think is more relevant to the company you are applying to. Remember, your advisor is there to guide you, not to do the work for you. They will be super impressed if you come to them with bullets like this, and hopefully, that allows for more time spent on chatting through your strategy for job applications (vs. writing a resume). Let's look at what the final set of bullets could look like.

Long version . . .

• Led customer segmentation project; generated insights to recommend next steps to get customers to buy from "insert company name" more frequently

• Analyzed customer data (using SQL, self-trained); recommend-ded including additional data sets to gain better insights (e.g., date of customer's first purchase, categories purchased, time since last order, etc.) and collaborated with the pricing/category teams on the final output

• Determined that shopping habits of top 20% of customers differ significantly than the rest; identified high potential customer profiles (from bottom 80%) and aligned on a product category "awareness" campaign to target them

Concise version . . .

• Led customer segmentation project; generated insights to boost customer repeat purchases

• Analyzed customer data (using SQL, self-trained); re-commended analysis method ideas, collaborated with the pricing/category teams

• Identified high potential customers not yet purchasing fre-quently; aligned on a marketing campaign to target them

Super concise version (if you want to highlight many other projects and need space) . . .

• Led customer segmentation project to boost repeat rates; analyzed data (using SQL, self-trained) while collaborating with the pricing/category teams; recommended a marketing campaign targeting high potential customers not yet purchasing frequently

Keywords that showcase multiple skills: Led, Analyzed, Self-Trained, Collaborating, Recommended.

Normally, all the recruiters I work with see is the word "Analyzed" or something similar and then a bunch of details on what the student did. If you still prefer to include all the details on the analysis to showcase your advanced experience with this skill, do it. But also do the version above. Get feedback from your career advisor on which version they think will work best with the specific employer you are targeting. If you get to develop rapport with a recruiter or employee from any company, get their feedback as well. The resume that works depends on who's reading it. From my experience, particularly with the larger and popular companies, a recruiter looks for red or green flags (GPA) and keywords that showcase multiple skills (both people and technical skills). Often students over-emphasize the technical skills. The above example is a way for you to differentiate your resume.

How to Get the Most out of a Career Fair

For almost all students (International and American), career fairs are put on a pedestal, meaning they are given a lot of importance. These fairs are treated as the end all be all way to get a job out of university. Students put a lot of pressure on themselves to perform well, especially with their first one.

For career fairs exclusive to undergraduates for entry-level positions, it's not uncommon to see lines of students waiting to get into the hall or even a line of students waiting to meet a single big-name employer such as Amazon or Google. Students' goals at these events are to get face time with an employer, have a conversation, hope they came across as hirable, hand over their resumes, and finally cross their fingers while waiting for a call or email back.

The generic advice students get about these events are things like smile, prepare to talk about yourself, do some research on the companies, make sure your resume is tip top. It's good advice, and you should do all of those things. But know they are the minimum bar for these events, the basics, not the high standard. The positive outcome from executing those basics is your resume ending up in the hands of a recruiter. But you are still left wondering if they will get back to you.

Let's say you hand your resume to 10 companies but spend only 1 or 2 mins talking to each (I've seen students just hand their resumes, say thank you, and walk away) . . . that would not be the best outcome in my opinion. The best outcome would be for you to:

1. Learn as much as you can about the companies you are interested in, and

2. Have 1 or 2 very good conversations with your top choice companies.

Let's break this approach down into details, and discuss why they matter. First, it's important for you to understand employers' motives from career fairs, to better plan and execute your approach.

Purpose of Career Fairs from the Employer's Perspective

In the previous chapter, we covered the hiring process and noted that career fairs are the top of the funnel, where employers cast a wide net to collect as many applicants as possible. There are a few considerations employers go through when planning to participate at career fairs.

First, they like career fairs because they typically get quality applicant leads. The leads they get are better than leads from random online applications. Think about it, anyone can apply online. It's fairly common for people to apply with bogus resumes, meaning the resume has inaccurate information (on background, degrees, skills, etc.). Employers have a hard time sorting through online applicants, to determine which ones are truthful or not, and which ones match the company's hiring criteria or not. And how would they know? It's not like they can cross-check resume information with student and employee databases from all universities or companies (they don't have access to those databases). Since career fairs limit access to a university's students, employers can tag the candidates they meet there as high-quality leads (vs. online applications) just because they know the resumes match the actual applicants.

Second, over time, employers figure out which universities produce solid candidates for the roles they need. Mid-size (1,000-5,000 employees) to Large (10,000+) employers typically have a campus recruiting team focused on establishing relationships with universities.

Companies can't physically be at every career fair in the country, so they must be selective. Students searching for a job are usually quick to learn about which companies frequently participate in their university's career fairs and what type of roles they hire for. Keep an eye on these companies, especially the ones you haven't heard of before (not giant brand names). Their intentions to hire from your university are higher than those from employers not participating in your university's career fair.

Third, the company needs to decide who they will send to represent them at the fair. There is no standardization as to whom companies send. They could send anyone from entry-level recruiters (people who recently graduated undergrad) to senior level recruiters, employees from different departments, or hiring managers. It really runs the gamut. Who they send depends on the size of their company, how new they are (startup vs. established business), and the roles they are trying to fill.

Here's an example to help illustrate this point.

Many companies now have leadership development rotational programs. These are entry level (some cases MBA level) positions, where a recent undergrad or grad student will get placed in different departments, typically over a one to two-year period. The idea here is to expose the student to different parts of the business, as those different parts might operate independently, but need to work together to make the company successful. At the end of the program, the graduate is placed in one of the departments full time.

The directors or senior managers that run these rotational programs are the hiring managers for these roles. They are typically full-time employees from non-HR or non-Recruiting departments. Over time, they get a sense of which students can succeed in these more ambiguous but exciting roles, and will often go to career fairs themselves to interview students. The typical process is for them to meet as many students as possible for a few minutes on day one, select the students they like, then try to do a more formal person to person interview with those individuals the next day (on campus). They want to leave campus with a good sense of who they want to hire, and they are typically quick to make an offer.

The opposite spectrum of this is an employer who sends a recruiter from their HR team to hire for 3 or 4 different role types. Those recruiters can't possibly be highly in-tune with what each role entails, or able to answer detailed questions about them. Their time and attention are spread thin, and the best outcome for them is to just collect resumes from applicants, knowing they are from a university that has produced solid candidates in the past. For you, even if you make a solid impression with that recruiter, it will only get you so far as they are not the hiring manager.

I hope this begins to clarify the difference between a hiring manager and a recruiter. Knowing who you are speaking with at a career fair is key. It all depends on who the employer sends, and what their goal is from the fair. By the way, it's not unusual for the big brand employers to send recruiters vs. hiring managers for entry-level career fairs. They just want to get a giant pipeline of candidates and then put them through the funnel. They will generate a large quantity of applicants as candidates are automatically attracted to their booth.

Steps to Achieving a GREAT Outcome from Career Fairs

Ever heard of the phrase "putting all your eggs in one basket"? Students often do that with career fairs. They think the fairs make or break it for them for finding a job. And because most students leave the "search for a job" phase to a few months before they graduate, they are late to the game and therefore psychologically lean more on the fair as their way to get an offer (you should be preparing to find a job soon after you start university!).

I'll argue that in this day and age, the majority of work to be done to succeed with getting a job is done outside a career fair. It's done online, via LinkedIn and email, through informational interview chats, and through referrals (when an employee recommends a student to a coop//internship//full-time role). I will cover these steps in detail in the Networking chapter. For now, let's discuss how to best make use of the face time you get at career fairs.

The absolute first step, is to agree with yourself on what a good outcome from the career fair will look like. As I mentioned, in my opinion, picking a goal of wanting to leave the career fair with a strong prospect of getting a job is not a good goal. It's too much pressure, and it doesn't match the bulk of employers' goals from the fair (they are in the collecting applications phase).

Finding a job is a longer-term process (it's a marathon, not a sprint), requiring you to research, build skills in writing and networking, etc. Use the career fair to research and practice communication skills. My suggestion of a GREAT outcome is for you to:

1. Learn as much as you can about the companies you are interested in, and

2. Have 1 or 2 very good conversations with your top choice companies.

First, before a fair, you will have access to the list of employers that will be there. Go through the list and read up on every single employer (you can exclude employers from industries you are sure you don't want to work in). Don't dismiss a company just because you haven't heard of them. You don't know what you don't know. Spend 5 minutes going to each company's website; look up their "About us" section, the "Products and Services" they offer, the type of "Customers" they service. Then type their name into google and select "News" to look at recent headlines they have made. All of this should take 5 mins per company, and it will give you a sense of whether you could be interested in them or not. Although you may want to work for a known name brand, so does everyone else. An alternate good option would be working for companies that aren't as well known, that provide services or products to other big brand companies. Those companies are typically smaller, so most of their roles likely entail more responsibilities than the same role in a larger company. This means you will learn more, faster. Those companies typically have a similar level of high-quality standards as the big brands, that's why the big brands selected to use their services/products. Bottom line, don't dismiss a company before you've spent a few minutes looking them up.

Second, select a handful of companies that are more important to you than the rest. For them, spend up to 30 mins reading on each to learn more. Besides the suggestions above, look up their competitors and how their products/services are differentiated (what their strengths and weaknesses are). Ask yourself why a customer or client would select this company's product/service vs. the competition's? Is it the price point, the features, or the way they take care of their customers after a purchase? Depending on what answers you come up with, ask yourself how it was that this company produced this differentiation. For example, if a company had the best prices in the market, it may mean they are more established and have built scale over time that has gained them better operational costs. If none of what I'm saying makes sense, invest some time researching business frameworks such as SWOT analyses and find examples of those frameworks applied to real companies. You also want to make sure you look up open roles on your target companies' career portals, and read up on the roles and departments they have openings in. As you go through this exercise for your top 4-5 companies, make a list of questions for each. You will use those questions to hold a solid conversation with a recruiter or hiring manager at the fair. Because you've done research, your questions will sound well prepared and intelligent, which will give off a good first impression.

Now, even though you've done a ton of reading to prepare for the fair (on all companies, plus in-depth work on your top targets), you can only learn so much about each. Here's the other thing, you can't possibly get a good sense of what each company really does just by reading. For example, a ton of marketing companies provide so many quirky online services, and even if you have a background in marketing, it can be very hard to understand what value they actually bring their customers - what actually is their product or service? However, a short conversation with a recruiter or hiring manager will likely explain what they do in simpler terms. These conversations will give you a better sense of what's out there in the market, what problems the different companies solve with their services/products, what type of companies or customers have a willingness to pay to solve those problems, etc.

Don't assume you know what you like if you haven't done a lot of this homework. Doing this homework and exposing yourself to these employers by asking them intelligent questions will get you closer to figuring out where your interests might be. Use career fairs to learn more about what's out there in the market and learn more about each of the companies that are hiring from your university. This is goal number 1. It's very different from the goal of "I need to find a job".

Goal number 2 is to have one or two very good conversations with any of your top 4-5 target companies. Generally, career fairs are a great place to practice having conversations. Key word here is "practice". I can't stress enough how important it is when going into these events to adopt a mindset of "I'm here to put myself out there, expose myself, get in an uncomfortable situation, practice my networking skills, practice just talking to people in general, because it will help me grow as a person, and get me closer to the person I want to be".

It's so hard to get yourself into that mindset if you add the pressure of "I really need to find that job now. Hope this career fair can help me". Pressure can be good, especially if you have prepared well. You have multiple tries to get it right . . . the career fair isn't make or break it. Start early. Take the career fair as just one more way to practice honing your communication skills. That's the mindset.

To prep for the day, be mindful of your energy prior to the fair. Do what you need to do to go to the fair in your optimal state (re-read the Energy section in Chapter 2 if helpful). In terms of how to dress, think about what you should be wearing, and then dress one level better than that. There is no harm in over-dressing in these situations. If you have no clue, for girls, put on a professional suit: pants/shirt/jacket or blazer (if you have it) or professional dress. For guys, put on a shirt and tie, non-jean pants, and if you have it, a suit jacket. You can't go wrong with that. Don't be lazy, do it. Look good and be proud of how you look that day. *You da boss.*

Now, you've done your homework on the companies, you have your questions on each company ready, you have your resume ready, your mindset and energy are tip top and ready to go, you look fly as hell . . . I already feel good about how this day will go for you ☺.

Start at the fair by using your non-top companies to warm up. It will help you build momentum for the rest of the fair. Go to the companies without a ton of (or no) traffic first. It's ok to take a moment to scope out the room, figure out where all the companies are located, and get a sense of which ones have a lot of traffic vs. ones that are more available. Remember the point is to practice having conversations, especially at the beginning of the fair. Select your first non-top company and start the conversation with this question "I've read up about you guys, had a few questions and was wondering if you can help answer some of them?". Note: I will not give you advice on how to say "Hi. How's everything?" and things like smile, and be friendly . . . you are all big girls and boys by now, I trust you have that down (if you don't, the career fair is not the first place you should be practicing that, join a university club or practice with your peers).

Now, as you are asking your questions, you want to practice keeping up the conversation and building rapport with the person you are speaking with. Do this by **listening** more than speaking. Then ask some more intelligent questions. If your goal is truly to learn more about their company, be able to come up with a few more questions on the spot, to keep digging (learning more) and to keep the conversation going. Another good goal in this conversation is to figure out if the person you are speaking with is a recruiter or a hiring manager or an employee from some department. Here's my favorite (tactful) question to ask: "I was wondering about the culture of the company, would you mind sharing how long you've been there, and what you like about working there?". If you feel they are opening up more when they are talking about themselves, ask them about what they don't like about working there, as well. This process should help you learn more about the company, about the person, help you practice your small talk and more importantly, warm you up for the next conversation.

Be mindful of two things, 1) there are other students there and if you find yourself in a line waiting to chat with a company representative, don't hesitate to start a conversation with a student (good practice), 2) if you are finding these conversations are draining your energy, take a break, walk around the room, walk out of the fair for a bit and come back . . . always be mindful of how your energy is, and manage it to better represent yourself in conversations.

Now, you want to do all this practicing and warming up while you keep an eye on your top 4-5 companies, to see when it might be a good time to approach them (when they are least busy).

I usually use one or max two conversations to warm up but find out what works for you. For your top companies, the goal is to avoid waiting in long lines, so you avoid (as much as reasonably possible) competing with others for the employer's attention. Also, try to notice if an employer has had a long series of back to back chats as their energy levels might be lower, and that will probably not lead to a good conversation. Look for openings where there are only 1 or 2 other students chatting with an employer. Use the same process above for your conversation: Start by saying you've been reading about the company and how they differentiate their products/services from the competition, and you are wondering what they think particularly makes them stand out in the market. If the company is super well known and that question about standing out in the market doesn't make sense, you can also ask something like: "I'm curious about a few open roles, have some questions about how they fit into helping the company provide more competitive features/pricing/support to their customers". Continue to follow the steps above, asking questions you come up with in the moment to learn more, and questions to get the recruiter/hiring manager/employee to talk about themselves so you can learn more about their role and build some rapport. If you come out of the career fair having one or two conversations that look like that, whether it's with your top targets or not, you had a good career fair. You learned more about those companies and practiced your small talk. It's a good achievement, believe me.

Now, to take it to the next level, you want to ask questions that allow you to follow up in some way with the company. Now that you've learned more about them, their specific roles, and more about the individual you are speaking with . . . you are in a fairly good spot to ask for something small from them. Say, "This conversation has been super helpful. I've learned a lot and feel more energized about pursuing a role here. In case I have more questions, would it be possible for me to follow up with you or someone else on the team, either via LinkedIn or email?". If they are excited by you, they may just give you their contact. If they give you their contact, and they are a hiring manager or employee, this is a super solid win (because in the follow-up, you can lead a conversation to a point where you can ask them to refer you). If they are a recruiter, they may be more hesitant to give you their contact, as they are on a mission to get many applicants and can't have them all follow up personally via email or LinkedIn.

Unfortunately, the common question students ask to close a conversation with a recruiter is, "Can you tell me more about the process to apply and next steps?". This also typically happens with no rapport or small talk up front. I often see students just say "hi" and jump to that question. PLEASE don't be that student! You are speaking with a human being. Even if it's their job to be there to answer your questions, they are human. They are susceptible to all the biases like the rest of us, and you will leave a bad first impression. Practice your communication skills. Always.

Another common mistake made by most international students is that they (without being prompted) ask the company representatives if they sponsor H1B visas. Some companies will flat out say no, others will tip toe around this as they may sponsor if they come across the right candidate. Ideally, students should have researched if those companies sponsor H1Bs ahead of time, by either checking with career services or researching online. If you are determined to ask that question at a career fair, at least start by building some rapport with the company representative first.

Now, if the recruiter/hiring manager/employee is not willing to offer a way to follow up outside the fair, then ask them about the process to apply and next steps. Because you followed the steps above first, you will still be 10X more memorable than the average student since you held a good conversation (vs. jumping straight into asking about a job). Hopefully, they remember you when reviewing applications after the fair, and you get a call or email to be invited to the next phase of interviewing.

Let's review the steps above on how to have a successful career fair:

- Get your resume in tip top shape
- **Read up on all participating companies, pick your top 4-5 and go into more depth to understand their business**
- **Log all the questions from your reading, to use for conversation at the fair**
- Dress up
- **Start your fair by warming up with non-top company targets**
- **Focus on building a connection, not asking for a job or a visa sponsorship**
- **Do that by asking questions to learn more about the company and the recruiter/hiring manager/employee**

- **Notice when talking to a hiring manager or employee (vs. a recruiter)**
- **Manage your energy that day, before and during the fair**
- **Look for an optimal time to talk to your top picks (avoid competing for an employer's attention as much as possible)**
- **If you have a good conversation, ask if you can follow up via LinkedIn or Email (especially if they are a hiring manager or employee)**
- If that doesn't work, ask what the application process looks like

The bold bullets are what you are doing differently from the average student. Do them. It'll be worth the effort and you will feel damn good about working hard to make the best out of the fair. The prep alone will make you stand out (first 4 bullets). Remember, if the only outcome is your learning more about the types of companies in the market (what they do) and having 1 or 2 good conversations (built rapport through small talk, found out more about the person you are talking to) . . . that's an awesome outcome. Pat yourself on the back. If you get a hiring manager or employee from one of your target companies to agree to follow up with you via LinkedIn or Email, you are a rock star! If you come out of it just having practiced some small talk, you should still be proud of yourself. It doesn't matter what stage you are in this process or what skills you still need to develop, what matters is that you keep making yourself a better version of you. And don't forget to be kind to yourself along the way.

Understanding Interview Dynamics

Interviewing is all about first impressions and selling yourself. It's about how you are perceived; not about how strong your credentials are. If you are invited for an interview, your credentials (GPA, major, experience) already passed the test.

Selling yourself and influencing how you are perceived is all done via communication.

So, what should you say? That's only part of what you need to work on. The other part is to actually have a conversation with the human being in front of you. If you just sit there, say "hi, how are you", and then answer the interviewer's questions, you might have something well prepared to say, but you are not having a conversation. When you just sit there answering questions, from an energy perspective, the interviewer is exerting much more energy to keep this conversation going than you are. Help take some of that work off their plate. And do it in a way that doesn't undermine the purpose of the interview OR the interviewer. When there is an energy balance in the conversation, e.g., they lead, then you lead, then they lead, etc., you will leave a good impression (assuming they liked what you said).

I've seen both sides of this spectrum. The more common approach from students is to be friendly and focus more on answering the interviewer's questions (making the interviewer do all the work). Even if that interviewer asks, "Do you have any questions for me", they'll get a standard, generic question like "What are the next steps for the interview process" OR "What does a typical workday look like in this role". Those are not memorable, not engaging, and still make the interviewer do all the work.

On the other side of the spectrum are students that are too assertive. This is less frequent, but I saw it often when interviewing students for sales roles. The extreme end of this side is a student who tries to lead the conversation frequently, talks over the interviewer interrupting them, and in some cases suggests that the interviewer is wrong by actually using the words "you're wrong" (there are more tactful ways to suggest someone may be wrong). Note: It's OK to suggest that you disagree with someone's thinking, argument, or conclusion (especially in the U.S.). But what I'm suggesting is doing it in a way that doesn't undermine the person you are speaking with. This student's example will be more memorable but not in a good way. They will be perceived as difficult to work with, and that is not the impression you want to leave.

Let's first dig into what to say in an interview.

Telling "Your Story"

The most common way an interviewer starts is with the question, "Tell me about yourself". The confusion for students here is "What specifically about myself?". "Should I talk about my background . . . my school experience . . . my work experience?".

My suggestion is all of the above. You want to connect with the interviewer. So, if you just answer their questions, and focus solely on relevant experience, it might not lead to establishing rapport. I suggest breaking out 3 stories; one from your personal life and background, one tied to your school experience, and one from your work experience (if you have some). Similarly to my suggestion on writing out many details on work experience for your resume, do that for your school and personal/background experience. Write at least one page for each (for your work experience, use the sheet you wrote for your resume). For each, focus on relevant details that highlight <u>key skills related to being dependable and successful at work</u>.

Example of a personal background story: "I grew up in a house with 4 boys. I was the oldest, so I got yelled at the most as my parents enforced most rules on me instead of my brothers. The house was frequently lively and loud, and we had to fight for attention from our parents and to get permission to do what we wanted. This experience reflects in my schoolwork, as I'm frequently one to engage with others or take the initiative to start something".

Again, you are writing this to tie it back to skills that are relevant to work experience.

Example of a personal, international background story: "I went to an international school in the U.A.E. I grew up with a variety of nationalities and religions, and would often celebrate Christmas, Eid, Diwali, Chinese New Year, etc., at school and at my friends' homes. I think this experience motivated me to travel more and led me to want to study abroad. This is likely why I often find myself easily engaging with any work group assigned to me for university projects".

This story naturally speaks to your ability and willingness to work with others. The other part of this specific example is that it highlights an international background. My advice is to never hesitate to highlight it if you feel compelled to do so. It is uniquely you, and a great way to differentiate yourself from others. I used to want to hold that side of myself back when I started working in the U.S., but later learned that it's my greatest advantage and a way for me to stand out. This was true for me both in my professional and personal life. Be proud of your unique stories and your background. I guarantee that once you embrace them, you will find they are a strength for you. Trever Noah is a GREAT example of a celebrity that embraces their international background in the U.S.

Here is an example of a school experience story: "Last semester was particularly challenging with the amount of work needed for each class. At times it seemed undoable. On one occasion, it led us to be severely delayed in delivering a group project for our statistics class. We agreed as a group that we needed to divide the work and set deadlines, in addition to asking the professor for an extension, which I volunteered to do. The professor hesitated at first, but I argued that the whole class may be in a similar situation, given the curriculum this semester. Ultimately, she agreed to push the deadline for all her students."

This story speaks to your communication and persuasion skills. On the surface, these stories may not seem relevant, but I'll say it again, they make the conversation more personal, and they are a great opportunity to highlight your non-academic (people-oriented) skills, which are key to what the interviewer is trying to filter for. Similar to the resume, the interviewer is trying to determine if you would be a fit for working at the company or on a specific team. Will you be able to work with your colleagues (people skills)? Will you be able to handle the types of projects that would be assigned to you (demonstrate this by speaking intelligently about your past work or school projects - don't forget to answer the "why" and "results" here). An interview is THE opportunity to elaborate on all the details you couldn't capture on your resume. Writing out detailed examples will help organize your thoughts on each of your stories, to best represent yourself in the interview. Remember, highlight a variety of skills, showcase your understanding of the projects you worked on, and what actions you took to make them successful.

Note on English speaking skills: Let's say one of the story examples above resonated with you, and you want to use it almost word for word in an upcoming interview. My suggestion is, DON'T. I'm indifferent to you using the story, but I encourage you to take the idea and say it in YOUR own words. It has to sound authentic.

Also, trying to sound too American, or as someone with strong

English language skills is not the goal here. All you need to do is get your message across clearly, accent and all. Do it your way.

Managing the Interview "Conversation"

Similar to the resume, you want to make each piece of the "tell me about yourself" stories into concise 30 sec to 1 min chunks. When asked "tell me about yourself", you want to speak for about a minute and a half to three minutes maximum. Remember, this needs to be a conversation. It's hard to have one if you are talking at someone and don't give them room to chime in. You don't have to tell every detail of your story up front. Leave them for the additional questions the interviewer will have. Spend about half of the time talking about your background and school experience, and the other half about your work experience (if you have it). In this upfront summary, you want to give the interviewer a very broad view of who you are and what you've done. Think of it as the table of contents for a book about your experience. Also, don't say the exact words on your resume! The interviewer can already see those. The idea here is for the interviewer to hear about you live from your own words, and then for her//him to dig into the areas they are most interested in.

Interviewers will have their standard follow up questions, like:

"Tell me about a time you used data on an analysis".

"Tell me about a time you faced a challenge with someone you worked with".

"Tell me about a time you overcame a challenge on a project".

They may use these standard questions, or they may probe into a particular part of your experience to get more detail. If you are really tuned into the questions you are being asked, you can get a sense of what SKILL they are trying to assess you on.

So, for the question "tell me about a time you used data on an analysis", they are probing on your *Critical Thinking and Intelligence skills*. They want to hear how you articulate what you did, to determine your level of understanding of the example you present. But, as always, this is an opportunity to demonstrate both those skills and your people skills. This is a chance to talk about how you thought about the problem, what tools you used and what the results were. It's also a great opportunity to talk about how you interacted with others on the solution; how you convinced your boss to include additional data criteria; how you coordinated with the marketing team on the next steps to execute a test campaign, etc.

When they ask, "tell me about a time you faced a challenge with someone you worked with", they are directly probing your ability to work with people. How you respond here is important. You want to show you confronted the situation (you didn't let it linger) and you worked out a positive outcome in the end. That's the basics. Make sure whatever you do to answer that question shows you took action and came up with a workable solution for you and the other person. Here's a tip for how to follow up your answer so it leads to a conversation with your interviewer. You could say, "While we (you and the person you had a challenge with) managed to find a workable resolution, it was admittedly a tough process" . . . say, "I can imagine this happens somewhat frequently at work. Any advice on ways to handle these situations better?". This may sound weird to you. But what it does is that it lets the interviewer talk about themselves, which is great for rapport building and allows for a conversation. This also helps balance the amount of talking, making the conversation better, and balancing the energy in the room (the interviewer will usually get energy when they talk about themselves or express their opinions, particularly when they are advising vs. informing you on a topic). It also shows the interviewer that you know that you are not perfect (guess what, she knows that, and she knows that most of the training you will need will happen on the job, not at school). It shows her you are constantly looking to learn and grow and that you are good at it because you have strong self-awareness (you recognize there may be better ways of handling that situation) and because you seek feedback to improve. Win-Win. Look for more opportunities in the conversation to get the advice of the interviewer (experiment with this if you have many interviews, you won't regret it). Just remember not to lose focus on answering questions (find the right balance).

On the question "tell me about a time you overcame a challenge", the interviewer is looking to see how you reacted to situations when there was some adversity. You want to describe the challenge, and then talk about how you successfully pivoted to make it work. You have a story for sure, and honestly, it can be one from work, school, or even personal life experience. If you choose a personal life example, make sure the story includes how you worked with people to turn things around to a good spot. Your work or school story should accomplish the same thing. Make sure you are always telling a story that demonstrates multiple skills, and that involves people skills.

Personally, one of my favorite stories to tell is related to sports. I have a story about a soccer tournament, where in the last minute before the tournament started, about half of our team bailed to form their own team. As the team captain, I had to scramble to find new players by making frantic calls to friends and literally walking around the tournament, asking other teams if they had spare players. If we couldn't get at least 7 players, we would be forced to forfeit. There was a lucky rain delay that bought us just enough time to find 3 new players, and when we played the (traitor) team who bailed on us, we beat them in an epic match (we defended the whole game, and scored the only shot we had on goal). It would have been easy to give up when we lost that many players, especially because there was no time to find new ones. But the rain saved us that day, and I learned that even if you are left with only one bad option, you should take it and try your hardest to make it work every time.

The point is, there are stories everywhere. Take advantage and find ones that give the interviewer a sense of who you are. Don't forget to make sure they highlight multiple skills along the way.

Finally, an interviewer will typically ask if you have any questions. This is a great opportunity to get them to speak not just about the company, but about themselves as well. Ask them the culture question, "I was wondering about the culture of the company, would you mind sharing how long you've been here, and what you like about working here?". She will likely talk about her role, different departments, what the people are like, etc. These are all great opportunities for you to probe and to show off your curiosity via intelligent questions. A great path to go down in this conversation, assuming you are speaking to the hiring manager or someone besides HR (unless you are applying for an HR role), is to dig into her role and the department she is a part of. Say "I'm trying to piece the puzzle together of how the different departments collaborate to give the customer a good experience with your products/services" . . . then say, "can you tell me a little more about what your department specifically does, and how it relates to the customer experience?". After she responds, follow up with "how do you collaborate with other departments to make that experience come to life for the customer?". You are getting the interviewer to be very specific with her experience vs. her answering a generic question about the company. This typically will get them more engaged in the conversation.

Other tips

As you've read above, dress up, prepare by printing your resume (multiple copies), bring a notepad and pen, and be on time! Manage your energy that day.

My personal energy management process is to sleep around 9 pm or 10 pm the night before, get up at 6 am and have a solid breakfast and coffee, bring a bottle or water with me to the interview, and for lunch (usually in the middle of the interview day) I'll only have soup. I find that if I eat as I would on a normal day (not particularly light), I lose a lot of energy the rest of the afternoon. The best part of my energy management is when I celebrate after the interview with a nice dinner ☺.

If you are interviewing via phone or video chat, you can prepare your notes in advance (your stories, information about the company, etc.) and have them in front of you during the interview (almost like a cheat sheet). If you are on a video call, you can put some key points you want to talk about on sticky notes and stick those notes on the side of your laptop or monitor window. That way, you can look like you are facing the screen while you take a peek at your notes. Honestly, if I were the interviewer and I found out you had a cheat sheet . . . I could care less. If anything, I'll be happy that you over-prepared for this interview. It shows you are committed and that you care.

A note on Visas

The situation with visas and permanent residence applications continuously evolves in the U.S. This has been especially true during the Trump presidency. It's really on you to stay on top of the paperwork required with visas, which can typically be a time consuming, non-fun activity.

Universities often bring immigration lawyers to talk about international student options and the latest in the news. Generally, visa specialists at your university and immigration lawyers have the most accurate advice on your specific questions (e.g., if you can delay or extend your program to buy more time to find a job). Start there with your specific questions and keep a lookout for when your university brings lawyers in for a talk. Take advantage of the free resource. Additionally, there are a ton of free resources online that explain visa options, and how they work. Websites like www.myvisajobs.com have comprehensive visa overview information and maintain a record of employers that have successfully issued these visas. A handy resource as you plan which companies to focus on with your job search.

6. Networking in the U.S.: How to stand out and beat the odds in finding a job

The Outcome you can expect from Practicing Networking

The thought of networking can be draining for many students, which makes the act of networking consume a ton of their energy. When something is that daunting, you have to have a good reason to do it. A purpose. And that purpose is usually to find a job.

But how does networking fit in the job search? Has anyone really connected the dots for you, explaining why networking is a MUST for your job hunt?

Universities will talk non-stop about networking and encourage their students to participate in their events, but I have yet to see someone paint a clear picture of why networking is that important. I've attempted to do that in a previous chapter but want to give it another try here.

At school (before college), you were either picked for a team (sports or otherwise) or you weren't. In some classes, the teacher liked you more than others, and sometimes they didn't. Certain students were your friends, others weren't. Of those students who weren't your friends, some were acquaintances (people you are friendly with, but don't necessarily hang out with) and some you simply couldn't stand (or they couldn't stand you). Life outside of school is no different in that regard. People will be people. They have their biases, they like who they like, and feel neutral toward or dislike others. None of these emotions are based on intentional decision making. It's all irrational and based on feelings.

With university applications, there is a more defined process for selecting which students get in and which don't. Universities liking or disliking you plays a very small role in your getting accepted. A big selection criterion is academic performance, your grades. Why? Because the university wants to ensure that by accepting you, you will actually succeed and graduate from their program. In other words, grades are a strong indicator of your graduating potential.

At work, there are ZERO guarantees you will succeed at a company in a particular team or role. Grades have very little correlation with a student's ability to succeed, and the CEO, VPs, Directors, Managers and HR team all know that. This forces companies to come up with other selection criteria, where grades play a small part of what is assessed, and which ultimately leads to *a lot of subjectivity in the selection process*. So yes, there is a lot of luck involved in your finding a role. You need all of the following things to happen at the same time for success:

1. The company needs to have open roles

2. You need to apply and hope they see your application

3. Your resume must check green flags (good GPA, major is in line with role) and the person or machine that reads your resume must select your application for the interview stage. If it's a person - Who are they? What's their mood when reading your resume? Are they able to remove biases as they read through it? Does their style match your style based on what you've written?

4. You must jive with the person interviewing you. Same challenges persist - they have their biases, and as much as they try to minimize them, they are only human in the end

5. And if you've made it this far, a few people at the company will compare your application with other candidates they liked and narrow the selection to make final offers

There are additional uninfluenceable factors that impact the above process, such as how many applicants the company gets for that role, how severe or lax the deadline is for filling that role, etc. You can say damn if you want to! Odds of getting a particular job are slim. Universities try hard to help you through this process by getting you job hunting resources, connecting you with recruiters (sometimes hiring managers) at career fairs, giving you a degree which is a pre-qualification for a job, etc. But that doesn't reduce the complexity or difficulty for students. Job hunting is really a journey that plays out differently for each person.

So, what can you control to improve your odds of success in this journey?

Start by working hard to get a good GPA. Apply to a ton of jobs, through career fairs and online. AND take advantage of there being subjectivity in how companies select candidates for roles. While on the surface subjectivity may seem unfair, you can (and SHOULD) turn it to your advantage.

Let's go back to the discussion about people being people . . .

In school, when your teacher liked you, or when your friend picked you to be on their team, it was because of their biases (they didn't make an intentional decision to like you, they were emotionally inclined towards you). You actually influenced them in one way or another to like you, even if you were not aware of doing it. Something about you jived with them. There is also an element of familiarity that's important. Sometimes, you may bump into someone who you knew from school, outside of school. Either at the mall or even later at university (where you discover you both have gone to the same university). You two are familiar to each other, so there is a natural inclination for you to try to connect in unfamiliar environments. Familiarity (or similarity) matters. Likability matters. And since finding a job is not just correlated to grades, and is influenced by subjectivity, likability and relatability matter, just like they did in school. Don't be fooled to think otherwise, this happens ALL THE TIME.

Many people don't get their jobs from simple merit (being qualified for them), rather because of connections. That is what networking is supposed to do, it's about establishing connections. More importantly, for finding a job, it's about **establishing connections in the search for advocates**. Advocates are people who would say, "Yes, I vouch for this person, I think they would make a good addition to the team". Since no company really knows the perfect formula for determining if a student will succeed in a role, when someone in the company vouches for a student, that goes a very long way in giving the company more faith they will succeed.

There are varying degrees of how someone can vouch for you. As an example, I refer people to roles all the time. People I know well and people I met recently (that have worked to network with me, that have done a good enough job of building rapport with me, and that are qualified for the role they are interested in). For the people I think are superstars, whether I know them well or not (could even be strangers, but they impressed me based on how they conducted themselves in as little as two phone conversations), I will usually print their resume and drop it on the desk of a hiring manager, adding a note this person is looking for a job and that I think the hiring manager will love them! It makes me look good for referring quality people, and if the hiring manager hires them, and the student turns out to be great (like I expected), I would have done them both a great favor.

Finding advocates is how you improve the odds of finding a co-op//internship or full-time role. Practicing networking is important now and even more important later in your career, as advocates will progressively be key to advancing your career. The earlier you start, the more career success you can expect now and down the road.

Search for Advocates

Advocates don't need to be strangers. In fact, the closer in relationship you are with a potential advocate, the better. Remember, an advocate is someone who is in a position to help you get a job, and is willing to vouch for you (like the teacher who liked you in school, or friends who picked you to be on their team).

This statement might be my most controversial in the book.

If you know someone who can easily put you in a role you want (or even a role you don't want), especially for your entry-level job, DON'T hesitate to take it. In fact, take it as soon as you hear about it. This person who's helping you could be a family member, a family friend, a business acquaintance of your Dad's, a cousin, an old colleague or friend, etc. It doesn't matter. Take the job and don't feel bad about it.

I'm not suggesting that merit doesn't count. If you have a good GPA, are hardworking, friendly, interested in improving your people skills, committed and ready to crush it on this job . . . all of that will come out with your work. Since getting a job involves a lot of subjectivity, even if you have all those good qualities, no one will have a chance to see them through the typical interview process. All they will see is how you present yourself (in person and in your resume).

As I mentioned in a previous chapter, some people understand the value of presentation, and prioritize practicing presenting themselves to boost their career. But how you present yourself does not equal to how you will perform on the job. So, take the job if it comes to you easily, understanding that there is an element of luck in the process anyway! Don't feel guilty, make the best of it.

Who is the Person you are Connecting with?

Knowing more about the person you want to connect with matters. If it is someone you know well, great! I'm not concerned with how you reach out to them. If this is someone you know of or is a complete stranger you found online or through your university, I advise the following steps.

1. Ask yourself: what do you know about them, and what can you find out?

Seriously, research them. Check out their LinkedIn profile to find out where they studied, what they studied, where they worked and what roles they've had. Google them. Read any interesting content you find, maybe something that highlights an achievement of theirs or a hobby they have. This matters because a key part of building rapport with your potential advocate is to get them to talk about themselves. One of my favorite ways to do that is by asking them how their career progressed to land them in the company and role they are in now. If you did your homework, the steps that got them to this company/role will be known to you via their LinkedIn profiles, which allows you to prep some nice questions to probe some more as they tell you their story. I love this question not just because it gets others to talk about themselves, but because I am GENUINELY interested in their story, especially the one about how they developed to get to where they are now. It helps me visualize my own path, and potential next steps I could take. Cultivating an authentic interest in others' career path and origin stories is an important part of adopting a growth mindset.

2. Ask yourself: How can this person help you?

This is to gauge what a good outcome might be from connecting with them. Asking yourself this question also helps you prioritize how important this person is in your networking search.

For example, is he in a role similar to the one you want, or is he a hiring manager for the role you want? Is she in the same department you wish to work with, or in a different but related department?

If he is in a similar role as the one you want, a good outcome might be that they like you and refer you to a similar role in their company. If she is the hiring manager, a good outcome is that she refers you and gets you started in the interview process ASAP. If he is in a different department, a good outcome is that he refers you to the department you want OR connects you (introduces you) to someone who works in another department of interest. In all cases, you will learn more about the person, potential roles, and the company in general.

3. Finally, ask yourself: How often does this person get contacted by people networking for a job?

If someone is in a position that's very important in a company (VP, Director, or more), they probably get contacted a lot. If someone is in an entry-level position or is a recent grad, they are less likely to be contacted often. Obviously, you want to connect with people who can quickly help you (someone with more influence, like a hiring manager). But since those people are contacted more frequently, you must factor that in. You can take a chance and contact them directly. You might get lucky, and it's good to experiment with this. Another approach is to talk to a few other people in the company first, to see if you can find a person who would introduce you to that hiring manager. That is a 10X more powerful approach, which will more likely connect you to your target person. More on tactics to establish connection with people later. For now, go through the questions above for each person (stranger) that you are thinking about connecting with. This will help gear up your networking approach.

What's in it for Them?

This question is so important for all aspects of your personal and professional career. This is about selling yourself and your ideas. It's about give and take. You will be asking your potential advocate to somewhat stick their neck out for you, so it's important to give them a good reason to do so. Give, then take, when possible.

With job hunting, it is unfortunately very hard to give and then take. You don't have much to offer at this early point of your career. If you recognize something that you can bring to the table, regardless of how small, you should take that opportunity to give back.

For example: later in your career, you will have random recruiters reaching out to you. They will ask if you are interested in a particular role they are recruiting for. People will respond to the recruiter saying yes or no. For those that are not interested in pursuing the role, over 90% will just respond with a "Not interested at this time, thank you!". If we step back for a moment, we would realize that it's a good thing the recruiter reached out. There is interest in our profile, and you can take advantage of this moment. I spend five minutes or less to make this recruiter's reaching out count for something. I ask myself what do I know about this recruiter? Are they an employee of the company they are recruiting for or are they a 3rd party contract recruiting agency? I may have interest in the company (might want to join them in the future), or if the recruiting agency is a strong one, it might be good to establish a connection with someone who works there. I've asked myself many times "What's in it for these recruiters?". I've spoken to a few I met on LinkedIn about "What's in it for them". They have a role to fill, they have a deadline to fill that role, and their compensation is tied to them meeting that deadline. Sometimes, their scope might just be to do an initial screening of potential candidates and then pass on leads to the HR team or hiring manager of a company. Either way, they are reaching out because they need you. So, what I'll do is respond with: "Thanks, but I'm not interested at this time. However, if I know of someone that may be interested, I'll send their contact your way. In the meantime, feel free to browse my network on LinkedIn for potential candidates, happy to make an introduction to someone with a profile compatible to your role". It takes me less than 5 mins to do the above, the recruiters are ALWAYS super appreciative because they rarely get that response, and I get to establish a connection which may be helpful in the future (plus potentially help someone in my network find a job). Win-Win. So, if you have an opportunity to give, do it.

But how will you know what to give? AND how will you spot that opportunity?

You have to understand the situation of your potential advocate to answer that. Ask yourself "What's in it for them?" Why should they respond to your LinkedIn note when you reach out? Why should they take the time to chat with you? Why should they connect you with someone else in their network? OR refer you to a role in their company?

I encourage you to think about these questions yourself, and to do so frequently. Here are my insights based on many years of actively thinking about this problem (how do you get someone to want something?).

For the recruiter or the HR employee, they are constantly searching the market for talent. Their jobs and livelihood depend on a continuous flow of new employees. Even in companies that aren't growing very fast, on average each company loses 5-10% of their employees every year. So, companies need a continuous flow of new hires, and they lean on their HR/Talent teams and external recruiters to lead that effort. When you reach out to them, remember that they are benefiting as their success with getting good talent into the company depends on finding candidates like you.

For Hiring managers, it's a similar story. They want someone strong on their team. They know the minimum qualifications for someone to pass their HR/Talent teams requirements, and they have a decent sense of who may succeed at the company. So, when you contact a manager, they likely will look you up (probably your LinkedIn profile) to see if there is any potential for you to be on their team. It's also likely they don't do that, or even respond. That is ok. What matters is that you have a sense of why they might want to talk to you, so you are on the same wavelength as them if you manage to start a conversation.

One other thing to note on hiring managers is that although they have a good sense of who might succeed on their team, they always have to manage the risk of bringing in someone who doesn't succeed. One way all hiring managers do that is by checking other managers' or employees' opinions on a candidate.

So, imagine if you worked your way to getting introduced to a hiring manager. The unsaid but obvious interpretation of a person introducing you is that they are in a way endorsing you to them, which makes you stand out as someone who has others within the company that vouch for you. Remember that when planning to contact hiring managers.

With regular employees in a role you want, who can introduce you to others, or who can tell you more about the company, they are generally just excited that someone is contacting them. Think about it. Your contacting them is a sort of validation they have achieved some status or some accomplishment by attaining a role that others want. For many, it's also a great opportunity to give back. Some of us genuinely want to help others and responding to someone who wants to learn more about our company or role is such an easy way to do that.

All of the above is a positive perspective of "What's in it for them". There are many reasons for strangers to not respond to you. The main one is laziness. They think, "Why bother?" This is a stranger and it won't do me any good to respond, I'm just wasting my time. This is reality and many people are like that. Don't let that discourage you and don't give those people more time than they deserve. As I mentioned, when you first get started, you might get 2 to 3 people to respond out of every 10 people you reach out to. That's assuming you reach out the right way. Once you improve your approach and can better prioritize who you reach out to, you can get to a 4 to 5 out of 10 response scenario. So, even when you get good, you still have a 50% chance of success. Knowing that should help you feel less discouraged when people don't respond. But as I mentioned above, there are plenty of "What's in it for them" reasons to successfully engage with potential advocates. Remember those and keep asking yourself that question.

Find or Create a Legitimate Starting Point of Connection

A "Legitimate point of connection" is about having a reasonable excuse to reach out to an individual.

You want to avoid contacting a stranger and saying, "Hi. I found you on LinkedIn and want to connect. Please add me", OR "Hi. I'm interested in exploring opportunities with your company. Please add me", OR just adding a stranger on LinkedIn with no context or communication.

There are two possible ways to contact strangers, you either have a legitimate reason to connect OR you create a legitimate reason to connect. Not having a good reason to connect is not an option.

So, what is an example of a legitimate reason? Meeting someone at a career event, after a presentation at your school, or being in a random professional webinar together (on LinkedIn or otherwise). In those scenarios, the companies are expecting you to approach them. The legitimate reason is they put themselves in a position to be contacted.

This also applies to family, friends, and peers. You have a social connection with them. You start from that point and then bring up the idea of how they might help advocate for you (if they are in a position to do that). Where this concept really matters is when reaching out to strangers. Let's say you did some digging and identified a person in a role/company you might be interested in. When you research that person, note what school/major/country/city they are from. You are searching for a similarity between you, which will serve as your legitimate starting point to connect.

Many universities boast about their alumni networks. The reason they do, is because they want to push you to leverage that network. You have a legitimate reason to reach out to people who have graduated from your school, under the pretext that you both have gone through similar training at the same school. That's a great starting point, which served me well when I applied for jobs after undergrad and my MBA.

If you can't find similarities between you and a person, you can reach out anyway, and by being extremely courteous, you will get some positive responses (I'll share many examples in the next section). But because you could not identify a point of legitimate similarity with those individuals, there will typically be less likelihood for them to respond. This is why starting your search with Alumni is the right first step (better chance of getting the ball rolling).

My approach here is to first find out how important this person is as part of my networking plan. Can I do without contacting them?

Or, are they the hiring manager of the exact job I want? If they are important to me, I will try to find a second person connected to them and who I have a stronger legitimate point of contact with. My goal here is to invest more time up front, trying to reach my target person, by getting a second person to introduce me. If this sounds insane to you, I don't blame you. It is what it is. The point I am trying to make is that no one is unreachable.

During my MBA, there was a student group dedicated to attempting a connection with absolutely anyone they chose in the world. They would outline who they wanted to reach out to, what the context would be, and would use the legitimate point of "We are a student body from this university reaching out to ask for your support with . . . [insert reason]". They connect with celebrities, presidents, sports figures, etc. If there is a will, there is a way. If it's important to you, you CAN make it happen.

How to Start a Conversation, Connect on an Emotional Level and Ask for a Referral - Even if You Are New to U.S. Culture

If it hasn't been made clear by now, the whole point of this book is to help you connect with others. As an international student in the U.S., this is the biggest challenge you will face. Nothing I write here will make a fraction of a difference if you are not putting yourself out there and trying to connect.

I've mentioned this before, but I will mention it again as I believe it is a core message of the book . . .

When you are first meeting someone in a professional context, focus on building a connection, don't ask for a job!

I can't stress the above point enough. 7 out of every 10 international students that contact me mention a "job" in the first note they send. My colleagues experience the same thing. Career advisors from top universities in the Boston area, where I live, tell me this is a common problem. Let's break down what the right approach should be.

The Initial Connection

I explained that asking a potential advocate for a job from the first interaction is like asking a stranger for $100. Odds are they won't pull out their wallet and give it to you. It's not a numbers game. No matter how much you try this with strangers, it will not work. It's like trying to fit a triangle-shaped object in a square hole. It looks wrong, and it feels wrong. Yet, so many students continue to introduce themselves in one sentence, then ask about a job in the second sentence.

This happens because students wait too long to start their job search. Suddenly, they find themselves three to four months from graduating and they search in panic mode. They have a "cut to the chase" attitude. They don't want to waste time networking, so they reach out to as many people as they can and just flat out ask about a role with their company.

You know, this isn't much different than dating. If you approach someone you are attracted to, flat out ask them if they would like to be in a committed relationship with you, and expect them to say yes just because you said hi and expressed interest, it's just not going to happen. It won't happen in the professional context either, so don't do it. Even if you are late to starting your job search, don't do it. Invest time in creating a connection first, then slowly but surely get to the point in which you can bring up your search for a job.

The other reason students get this wrong is that they *don't know what else to say*. They think the point of my reaching out is to talk about a job, so I should say that upfront. No. That's not how it works here. You need to use a different, lighter approach when you reach out. At one point, when you become gangster good at this, you can use a more direct approach. At that point you will succeed because you will know who to approach, you would have set up the exact context that maximizes the odds of them responding to you, and you will know exactly what to say to lock them in.

When students are told they need a non-direct approach, they get stuck because they don't know what to say. And they don't know what the steps are to get from an initial contact to asking the person to be an advocate for them.

So, let's look at the steps and some examples for the initial connection:

1. Once you've identified your potential advocate, softly introduce yourself using your legitimate point of connection as justification

2. Ask for an informational interview, and promise them it won't take over 20 mins of their time

3. Be courteous by acknowledging that they are busy and that it's ok if they can't spare the time

Real-life Examples of an Initial Intro

As you read through each example below, try to decide if this was a Good or a Bad example of an initial outreach. When it's hard to tell, think of what parts of the note you thought were good, and which parts can be improved. All of the examples are from international students.

Example 1:

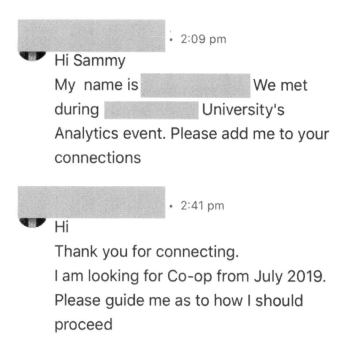

What do you think, good or bad?

This student's intro includes a key element of an initial note - a legitimate point of connection - that we were at the same event where I was a panel member. Even though I didn't chat with any students after the event, it's still a legitimate point of connection. Good so far. The student asked me to add them to my connections . . . ok, cool. Not sure why I should add them, but I get it. They are new to this, and I'm a nice guy, so I'll add them.

The takeaway is <u>you should explain why you want to connect</u>. Just asking to connect doesn't make sense. They could have improved the first note by saying, "I'd love to connect as I'm building my network of professionals in the tech industry and may want to reach out in the future if you would be open to that".

Once I connected, the student followed up with a note within an hour, mentioning their intention of "looking for a co-op, guide me how". As I said, this is what the majority of notes I get look like. PLEASE Don't do this! Don't ask about a job in the initial note to a stranger. It's too direct and rubs people the wrong way. More subtlety and patience are required. I still give credit to the student for being brave enough to reach out. I know it's not easy, especially when you are first getting started. To improve and get results, they must work on their approach.

Example 2:

• 6:20 pm

Guidance regarding full-time opportunity (Procurement) at ▓▓▓▓▓

Hi Sammy,

Glad to find a Penn State alumni at ▓▓▓▓▓

I am a second year MBA student at Penn State University with a concentration in Supply Chain. I have around eight years of experience in procurement/supply chain prior to my MBA. I want to connect with you to get your guidance regarding applying for full time procurement opportunities at ▓▓▓▓▓. Let me know if it is possible for you to spare some time to guide me about the same. Looking forward to speaking with you.

Please find attached my resume for your reference.

In this example, the student was definitely more polite, less curt than the previous example. They did, however, make the #1 mistake all students make by asking for a job in the first note. They actually put their intention as the title of their note

"Guidance regarding full-time opportunity". Again, this is off-putting, right off the bat. Understand that experienced professionals get these notes all the time. Why should they help you get a job? They know nothing about you yet. Don't ask for a job from the initial connection, and especially don't include that in the title of your note. Moving on . . .

The student used a legitimate point of connection - they are studying their MBA at the same school I did my undergrad in. I didn't do my MBA there, I studied Electrical Engineering. So, my experience was different, but still, it was appropriate for the student to mention that as a point of connection. They go on to explain more about themselves - 2nd year MBA, 8-year experience in supply chain . . .This is good, but I still know where this is going. They are asking me for a job. The student then asks about a full-time role, and that they want to chat with me. They also attached their resume!!

Why should I read their resume or feel compelled to help them? They haven't even given me a good reason to get on a call. Also, they are asking me to commit a lot. If I got on a call with them, I know I would feel obliged to spill my guts with information that would help this student figure out how to apply. But what if I don't think they would be a good fit for the company, should I help them anyway?? It's too much pressure. They have already drained my energy with their note.

The other part they missed was that I'm not in operations or supply chain, but they are looking for those types of roles. That information is in my LinkedIn profile. This is a mismatch, so in any case, I would have been most helpful by telling them the little I know about that department, and potentially connecting them with someone who can help more (who works in that area). You, the student, have to tease out these details and use them in your strategy and approach when networking. It will make you stand out.

This student was at least considerate of my time by including the phrase "if I can spare some time to chat". While that was better than example 1, it's still not good enough. This is another bad example.

Note: I did respond to the student and helped them. I do it mostly because I remember what it was like to be in their shoes. But when I respond to poor notes, I always coach on how to have a better approach the next time they contact a stranger. If you get feedback from strangers, take it seriously and learn from it. While they may come across as harsh for being so direct ☺, it takes energy from them to do that, and the only reason they do it is to HELP YOU. Feedback is a sign of someone wanting to help. Remember that.

Example 3:

> ████████████████   • 12:52 pm
>
> **Penn State MBA graduate seeking your expertise**
>
> Hello Mr. Hejazi,
>
> My name is ███████████ and I am a recent MBA graduate from Penn State Smeal College of Business- Class of 2019. I am currently exploring full time roles in supply chain and trying to learn more about supply chain/operations roles at ██████
>
> Can we connect sometime to discuss your experience at ██████? Your insights would be really beneficial to me.
>
> I know you're busy and your time is valuable. If you have a few minutes, I'd be really grateful. If not, I totally understand – no worries!
>
> Thank you for your time

Let's start by looking at this student's note subject. They get it. They are seeking expertise. What they are indirectly saying by including this title is "Sammy, you clearly have advanced in your career, I'd like to chat with you about that". I promise this has nothing to do with ego. It's just that so many notes are about looking for a job, that it makes this approach feel refreshing. It takes the pressure off.

The student says more about themselves, that they are exploring full-time roles, but that their intention with me is to learn more about my experience and insights, not how I can help them apply. Love it. It's subtle, and it keeps the pressure on me low. They then highlight I may be busy, that my time is valuable, and that they would be grateful if I can chat (they also say it's ok if I can't). They made me feel not obliged to do anything. They were also super courteous throughout the whole note. You should honestly steal the last two paragraphs in this example and use them anytime you try to connect via LinkedIn or email. It's very refreshing compared to the typical note.

If anything, this student could improve their note by mentioning how I might help them given that I'm not in a supply/chain or operations role. They could say something like "understanding you are in a different area within the company, I'm looking to understand how you may interact with Ops/Supply chain, to gain deeper insights vs. what I can find from articles and your website".

By the way, I had several conversations with this student and connected them with someone who works in Ops. This is a good example.

Example 4:

· 11:29 pm

Hello,

I hope you are doing well.

I am currently working California (Silicon

and this internship started from 1st July and would end by 30th August. Furthermore, after that I'm available for internship/co-op (in the domain of data analytics and business intelligence) from 14th September 2019 through December 2019 full-time. If you can kindly help me in this case, I would really appreciate it. I can send you my resume if you want.

I look forward to keeping in touch and staying connected. It would be a great pleasure to hear back further from you. Thanks and Regards,

Sammy Hejazi · 8:21 am

Hi

I can help with full time roles. Find 2-3 open positions you are interested in and I can refer you to them.

Best

· 9:56 am

Ohh, okay. So, currently, I'm looking for intern/co-op role but when I would be looking for full-time role, I would definitely let you know sir. Thank you so much.

· 9:58 am

So, for full-time roles, I should let you know the openings which are in only right? Or you can refer me in any other company too (where you have your other business contacts and referrals)?

I look forward to hearing from you at your convenience.

By now, you should be able to spot what doesn't look good in introduction notes. In this example, I'm showing you a full conversation thread. The student doesn't use a legitimate point of connection to start the conversation. First mistake. They went to the same university I did my undergrad in but did not mention it. Second, they gave me a lot of detail about their current internship (when it started and when it ends). This is all irrelevant to me at this point. They haven't mentioned their intention yet, but I can already sense this is about asking for my help with a job. They then tell me about the exact dates they are available for a co-op. I'm not sure why they have targeted me at all . . . do they want me to help with a co-op?? Nothing on my LinkedIn profile suggests that I can help here. Co-op and intern candidates at large companies are typically vetted by the talent/HR team, and I don't work for that team. So far, this student has really missed the mark.

However, I will add that they were extremely nice and polite in the note. It doesn't go unnoticed. I know that it's hard to find the courage and energy to go through this networking process and appreciate that students are going through these emotions. But still, not good enough.

I replied back and explained that I'm willing to help with full-time roles. I do this because I want to give back as much as I can, but normally the way this student's note is written would not get a response (they will need to work on their approach).

They are appreciative, even if I can't help with a co-op. The student then continues by asking me to clarify what I meant when I said I can help them with full-time roles. They ask me if I meant that I could help them with roles within my company, or if I could

help them with any role in any company where I have contacts ...
☺

What am I supposed to do with that?

This is as if they are asking me, a total stranger, for $10,000. What have they done to establish that kind of relationship, or even rapport with me? I share this example to help you learn what not to do. I understand that students experience a lot of confusion when they are starting to practice networking, so I take none of the notes personally (and I still helped this student). Seriously though, I hope this example serves its purpose of reminding you how important it is to establish rapport first when networking. Again, don't ask for a job, build a connection.

Example 5:

> · 4:34 pm
>
> Hi Sammy;
> I am an INSEAD alum of 16D, and I am
> interviewing for R2 with ▮▮▮▮ for a
> Senior Category Mgr role. I was
> wondering if I could touch base with you
> to learn more about the role/company.
> Let me know if any particular time works
> for a call, I am relatively flexible.
> Warm regards,

Here's another simple, good example. This student is already in the application process, and wants to learn more. I messaged back and forth with them for a while. The key for the initial outreach note is to ask to "learn". An informational interview is a light ask. Anything else is too heavy in the beginning.

Example 6:

Sammy Hejazi · 4:26 pm
Hey ⬜⬜⬜ Im a 17J graduating in July and will be applying to positions at Google in Mountain View. I would love to pick your brain about your role and and the company in general, If you can make some spare time. Any help/advise would be appreciated. Thanks!

⬜⬜⬜ · 4:28 pm
Happy to chat. Drop me a line
⬜⬜⬜

This was a note I sent during my MBA. I sent this to a complete stranger, who worked at a target company of mine and who was an alumnus. My just mentioning that I'm a 17J (INSEAD lingo for "graduating class of July 2017"), while knowing that they are an alumnus, is enough to signal that we went to the same school. Here I was more bold than usual and highlighted that I will be applying to open roles. However, I didn't ask them for advice on how to do that. I asked to "pick their brain about their role and the company," not about applying to a job. It's a subtle but very important difference. It lowers people's defenses. They don't feel tied to an outcome or pressured to do something for me. They are just committing to a short conversation where they will talk about themselves (something most people love to do). If you ask for help with applying to a job, it puts people's defenses up. I hope I have repeated this point enough times by now ☺.

The First Conversation

Here's what to do when you get someone to agree to a chat.

One, treat this conversation as if you are being interviewed. Meaning, be on your best behavior and be polished overall with what you say. If your style is to lean on being more casual, that's ok. My point is that you should work to impress this person. They agreed to chat with you, but they don't owe you anything. You are working to encourage them to become an advocate for you, so you want them to like you.

Two, be genuinely interested in the person's background, their career progression, their role and the company. Genuine interest means you are trying to learn from them, and because you have done your homework, you know what specifically it is that you are trying to learn. Let that curiosity come out in your questions. Since you have a short amount of time to chat, you want to make sure you get as much information as possible. So, you want them to do most of the talking (75% them, 25% you). I've definitely experienced the reverse of that, almost like the student was auditioning for me. Remember, the idea is to treat this conversation "as if" you are being interviewed, but IT IS NOT an interview. Be on your best behavior (as you would be on an interview), but don't do most of the talking. This approach also encourages your potential advocate to become at ease and to talk about themselves. Usually, a smart move when building rapport with someone new.

Three, look for opportunities to build a "connection". Many, many books are written on this subject . . . there is that much content out there. The summary on how to build a connection is to **_search for similarities using small talk_**. You want them to like you, to "feel" that way.

Feeling something is not logical, you can't reason your way to creating that emotion in others. But you can encourage others to lean towards liking you by helping them perceive similarities between you two. Work to discover those similarities. Since people like to talk about themselves, find ways to give them an opportunity to do so. The technique here is to bring something up about yourself first, which should encourage your potential advocate to reciprocate and say something personal in return. If you were American, you might talk about football or what state or city you are from.

So, what should international students talk about?

My favorite basic technique is to talk about trying new food or travel. The idea with those two topics is that any individual on the planet typically has to put themselves out of their comfort zone to experience those things. So, people experience food and travel in a similar way.

When you try new food, it's hit or miss, so it's always an adventure. When you travel, you are putting yourself where you don't know exactly what to expect. You can talk about your school experience, especially if your potential advocate is an alumni, however, if they are American, know that they likely experienced school a little bit differently than you have, and the idea is to chat about something that exposes similarity (but also makes them "feel" the similarity). The school topic is good but isn't my favorite. If you have stories from school you found help build a connection with American alumni, fantastic! Use those stories with any new potential advocate you meet.

Going back to food and travel, if you are talking to an alumnus, you can talk about where you have been going most frequently to eat out. Your potential advocate likely had their go-to places when they were at university, and that could start up a small conversation about good places to eat. You can also talk about how you've searched for a restaurant that serves dishes from your home country, and how they are ok but not great. You can mention what makes a dish authentic (e.g., the right spices, or sauce, or vegetable) and give advice on how to spot that anytime they are in a restaurant that serves those national dishes. On travel, you can bring up your most recent trip within the U.S. It doesn't matter if that trip was local or out of the city or state your university is in. Talk about what you liked AND what you didn't like from your visit (talking about what you didn't like makes you appear more real; it helps with bonding). Perhaps you are trying to plan a trip, you're not sure where to go, and can ask them for advice on their favorite places in the country. They will love that question, and will likely have a lot to say. Remember, you want to get them talking more than you are . . . keep the 75% them, 25% you in the back of your mind.

Once you have more practice with these basic small talk ideas, you can graduate to a much more powerful method where you are being your authentic, genuine self without reservation. The more you interact with Americans, or anyone from any country, you will realize there are basic emotions we all experience similarly. It doesn't matter if those emotions were created in Delhi, Dubai, Shanghai, Mexico City, etc. If you can convey a story that highlights basic feelings, it will resonate with any person you are trying to build rapport with.

The tactic here is to have stories about yourself from your home country, or from an adventure you had (including the one where you came to study in the U.S.). You can think about one or two meaningful stories to you, that excite you or that drum up a lot of emotion and write them down to start. Practice telling them to friends, professors, career advisors or anyone with whom it's ok if the story doesn't resonate perfectly. They are your opportunity to fine-tune your craft. Once you are comfortable enough, they are a great way to build rapport with strangers as they show your sincerity and vulnerability (because they are personal).

I like to tell the story of how I ended up at Penn State.

"In high school, I had ZERO ideas about where to apply to! It was even tough to figure out that I wanted an Engineering degree, let alone pick which school to leave my whole world for. All I was sure of was that I wanted to leave the U.A.E., and figured the U.S. was a good option. My parents weren't so sure that was a good idea but supported me. My dad did his master's degree at the University of Michigan, so I set my heart on going there. I was advised to apply to other universities in case I didn't get in, so I literally asked my friends where their older brothers and sisters went. I could have found info online to make a more informed selection, but I was more comforted by the idea of going somewhere where someone like me (from my High School) had gone before. I applied to Penn State and University of Illinois. It hit me quickly that those choices would only land me in states that were cold. That wasn't good. I like warm, sunny weather. In my mind, my only options for that were California and Florida, but California was too far away, so I applied to Florida State University (the first option that came up when I searched Florida Universities online). Ultimately, I got accepted to 2 schools (Michigan wasn't one of them, but I never say that in my conversations), and I basically did eeny, meeny, miny, moe to select Penn State."

People, including Americans, can relate to the tension and anxiety that exists when selecting which university to attend. What I found from practicing this story with alumni from Penn State, was that more than a few Americans from Pennsylvania knew basically from birth they were going to Penn State. Their parents went there, and they have been going to their football games their whole life. While this story didn't highlight similarities between potential advocates and myself, it shows the bold decision-making international students typically face during this part of our lives. Americans aspire to be bold. Everyone wants to be *Indiana Jones*. This story gives them a feeling of how international students did just that by coming to the U.S.

Finally, you want to keep asking yourself, "Why should this stranger be MY advocate?". Why you and not someone else? You need to understand that you've already done a lot of good things to deserve it being you. You took the initiative to reach out. You did your homework on the person and on the company. You asked great questions and showed genuine curiosity. All of this shows your smarts and determination. I've often interviewed people who made it past the resume stage, who told me this job isn't their first choice . . . what a put off and a waste of time that is. I mention this to give you a sense of what we (hiring managers, recruiters) experience in the real world. So, seeing someone that is determined and smart is nice. You want to make them feel like you would be a good addition to the company (that's why I say treat these initial conversations as informal interviews). Do your homework on the person and on the company. Practice your stories, make a good first impression with your first note to potential advocates because these steps add up to help you stand out as a job candidate.

At the end of your first chat, you want to conclude by asking if it's ok to follow up if you have additional questions. Post chat, send a note thanking them. And if you are an absolute baller, recap what you chatted about. Highlight the key take away learning points you got, and what you are thinking about doing next in your search (e.g., how you plan to talk to other companies about how they approach supply chain, etc.). This leaves a great impression since you are showing you manage your chats and yourself well . . . which makes you appear to be a great addition to any company. Trust me, do this. More importantly, get on many calls with potential advocates and start practicing, and then practice some more.

Following up

You want to follow up with your potential advocate if you believe there is value in doing so. At the end of the day, you are going through all of these networking learning pains to get better at it and ultimately to find a job. So, you will always have a reason to follow up. Just make sure your reason fits in with the conversation you had with your potential advocate (remember the example when the student asked me if I can refer them to any job in the world? Don't follow up like that). For example, you may have realized from your conversation you need to speak to someone else in the company (maybe someone in a different role or department). It makes sense then to follow up on your initial conversation letting your potential advocate know how your thinking has evolved since the conversation (e.g., that your interest is leaning more towards this other role or department) and that you are wondering if they would make an introduction to connect you with another employee in their company. Explaining your thoughts, and how you arrived at your decisions, is generally appealing and gets people engaged.

Another example would be if you and the potential advocate actually built some rapport during the conversation. Like I mentioned several times, you will meet people you jive with. With those folks, I try to establish more of a mentorship relationship where I will reach out when I have a question I need help with. I'll ask them for advice on my career, on what I'm thinking I want to do, on what my approach is, etc. You can usually tell who you jive with by noticing how frequently they respond to you and how much information they offer when they speak with you. If their hand is a very giving one, use this opportunity to learn more from them (vs. asking them to help with a particular job application). Build the long-term relationship. Now, if the person you spoke with is the right person to refer you to a role you are interested in, you should go ahead and ask them for that help.

I'll argue that the fact that you did a ton of research on them and their role/company, that you reached out, set up a conversation and had a good productive chat, and followed up with a note recapping what you learned and your next steps . . . you then have done the *BARE MINIMUM* to allow you to ask them to refer you to a job.

You have checked enough boxes for it to be socially acceptable to ask for a referral. You could do more by finding other excuses to chat with them and continue your conversation first . . . but my advice is if you want to go for it now, it's only fair. You've done enough work, nice job. Here's how to ask them.

Getting the Referral

Follow up with them anywhere between 3-7 days from your phone conversation. Send them a note via LinkedIn or email saying:

"Hi [insert name], hope all is well. I've given our conversation from a few days ago some thought, and based on your insights, I'm feeling excited at the idea of a supply chain, large parcel analytics role. Understanding that we only met briefly, I'm wondering how you would feel about potentially referring me to a couple of roles that I'm interested in? I'm hoping this is a low pressure ask for you and respect your decision either way. If it's not something you can support me with at this time, I totally understand. No worries :). Thanks again for the conversation the other day".

If they don't respond in 2-3 days, send them a reminder.

One note to point out on reminders, don't send them at the end of day Friday or during the weekend (at least from my experience, I've found those times to be off-putting).

If they respond and say they can't help you at this time . . . thank them, and move on with your search.

The note asking them to refer you is effective only after you've done all the work upfront and had an initial conversation with your potential advocate. Without that work, just don't. Please put in the work.

Keep an eye out for Mentors

Mentorship serves different purposes, and most people talk about these two forms of mentors: Coaches and Sponsors.

Coaches are what most students normally think about when it comes to mentors. This is someone, typically with more experience than you, who advises you on your approach with a problem you are trying to solve. I mentor many people in this way. We have 30 min chats every 6 weeks, where I ask about how they are doing, what's top of mind for them, and if I can help advise them on any particular topic. This last sentence sounds canned . . . all of that does happen but it's much more fluid and conversational. I also have people who coach me. They are not formal mentorship relationships; meaning, we don't officially put a label on our relationship as mentor and mentee (although other advice out there will suggest that it's important to make it official), but I look up to these people as mentors or coaches. I'm sure they view our relationship as one where they are helping me progress in my career.

I enjoy conversations with them. There are many examples where I have gotten great ideas on how to execute my projects, and I follow up to continue to get their advice and refine my work. For me, it's all about them helping illuminate different options I had not thought of myself. When someone has travelled a path, experienced it, and knows where the turns and pitfalls are, they typically do a good job when they coach others on that same path. I take their advice and their comments seriously. I also watch out for when their advice misses the mark (when they talk about something they don't have much experience in).

A good coach or mentor will tell you when they don't know. A really good one will help you think through how you might approach solving your problem, by asking you a lot of good questions (they don't have to know the answer, but they know how they would think about the problem if they had to face it themselves).

The advantage of having these relationships is that you can have a few people to ping about something you are working on. It reduces the guesswork and the chance of you making mistakes. Over time, it helps boost your career progression vs. those that don't have people advising them frequently.

The second mentor type is a sponsor. A sponsor can open doors for you. Your relationship with them would be more formal than with a coach. You would treat them more like someone you need to impress. These are people who are usually much more senior than you; therefore, they have the leverage to open doors for you when the time is right (and if your relationship with them has evolved to a stage they would consider doing that for you).

A mentor can be a peer, a professor, a senior person at your company, a 2nd cousin, etc. You don't have to look too far for them. You just have to pay attention. A mentor is typically someone with more experience than you in some dimension AND has taken some sort of liking to you (you clicked with them). A common cue to spot a mentor is when someone frequently gives you feedback. Feedback is typically viewed negatively. But, it's actually super positive when someone keeps giving you feedback, as their intention is likely that they want to see you improve. Another queue is someone who regularly checks up on you. They might say hi more frequently than others, or ask how you are doing and what you are working on even if they can easily get that update from your boss or otherwise.

If you are not experiencing any of these cues, put yourself in situations where you might meet people with more experience than you. Join a club or a group you are interested in. People there have experiences that are varied and you'll likely meet people you can learn from. Don't shy away from groups related to culture, like Asian or Middle Eastern, etc. Take advantage of the fact that you have that similarity to engage, and keep an eye out for people you click with (whether they have more experience than you or not). If they have more experience, and you want to develop a mentorship relationship, don't hesitate to ask them if they would be up for a coffee chat. Use your networking and communication skills to help start those conversations and develop them into relationships. If you are not confident in your skills, do it anyway, that's the only way to practice and make it work for you.

Some tips for organizing your approach to mentorship relationships:

Start a spreadsheet and make a list of all the potential or current mentors you have. Add columns for "Relationship" (where you know them from) - "Importance" (how senior are they, what doors can they open for you) - "Last Contact" (the date you last spoke with them) - "Context" (capture the notes from all your conversations). This should help keep you organized and keep the idea of mentorship top of mind for you. For those folks that are more important, set an agenda for each time you meet with them detailing what you want to discuss, and share it with them before your meeting. Towards the end of your meeting, ask them if they need help with anything and offer your time (to support them). After the meeting, follow up with a note thanking them for their time, and recap what you chatted about and what you are planning to do next. If some mentors are becoming less responsive, or pushing off meetings frequently, let them go, it's ok. You don't have to keep pushing to keep those relationships alive. If something comes up, down the road, where you could use their help, definitely reach out. You don't have much to lose at that point.

Ultimately, with or without mentorship, you are responsible for your professional success.

If you are determined, you will succeed, and you might even surprise yourself with the extent of your success. What mentorship offers is ***increased speed to success***. To give this thought more color, I like to compare mentorship to "hints" when playing video games or solving a puzzle. When stuck, you can spend countless minutes or hours trying to move to the next level OR you can get a hint. If your game or puzzle doesn't offer you a hint, in this day and age, you can go online (Google or YouTube) and you will likely find your hint. When you cultivate a network of mentors, it's like having a cheat code (hints) for your professional career. Remember this as you progress on your journey.

7. Thriving in the American workplace: Practical steps to put your best foot forward in your co-op or internship

This chapter is meant to give you guidance on how to approach your first American workplace experience. Landing a co-op or internship is possibly the best way to experiment and learn about the American workplace because it is OK if you fail or mess up. All international students with an opportunity in their academic calendars to get work experience prior to graduating should prioritize that over taking additional classes. The content below paints a picture of what to expect and helps with generating ideas for what you might want to focus on and experiment with, during your co-op or internship.

To Succeed in the American Workplace – Speak Up More Often

Understanding American work culture will take time. It won't become clear until you experience it. Typically, Eastern, Indian, Middle Eastern, and Latin American cultures are very hierarchical. Also, academic institutions are very hierarchical -

your teacher is the boss. Overall, your experience growing up at home was probably also very hierarchical with lots of rules about what you could and couldn't do. A common outcome for individuals from hierarchical cultures is they speak only when spoken to (in class or in a professional context). They often don't give themselves permission to speak up at will.

In the U.S., the general idea is that everyone is accountable to everyone else, so hierarchy takes on a bit of a different meaning. It is more acceptable to disagree openly with others, than it is in most other cultures. For example, the press can question the president and push back if they disagree. A VP in a board meeting can disagree with the CEO on a topic. Are there repercussions? Probably. Is it an absolute given death sentence to go against your boss or the authority? NO. And you can reduce the probability of any repercussions based on "HOW you disagree". The way you do it matters.

In day to day business, in most American companies (particularly new ones, progressive ones, and ones in new industries), it is expected that you voice your opinion. You can't nod yes to something you don't agree with (just because someone important said it). If you disagree, you have to say something. If you say nothing, it's the same thing as agreeing. More traditional companies in the U.S. (ones that have been around for a while and kept their same leadership team, like those in the Oil and Gas industry), may have a more hierarchical, political culture. You will have to assess what the situation is wherever you end up doing your co-op or internship. Either way, with traditional or progressive companies, you will have to speak up more than you are used to (it will feel uncomfortable at first, but it's part of the American learning experience).

If you are in a meeting and the topic relates to your work, and you have something to say, always say it. It doesn't matter if it's a question or an opinion, not talking in meetings at an American company is unacceptable. Everyone is expected to contribute. This is counter to a lot of international workplace cultures, where many people attend a meeting but are not expected to speak up. In fact, they are expected to not say anything unless someone senior asks them to. If you are new to this dynamic, I suggest speaking up, while trying not to say something too controversial. If you feel your idea or question might be a hot topic, find another thought or question to ask that is less controversial (at least until you build up your credibility with the people in the room). Use your best judgement regarding what to say.

Additionally, individuality is a big part of U.S. culture (socially and professionally). Your boss and peers will watch you, to size you up. They want to figure out who you are and what your personality is like. In most companies, they introduce new hires by asking them to say 3 things about themselves (fun facts typically), to showcase their individuality. How you are perceived carries you a long way with succeeding in the American workplace. You need to manage it. Here is how to do that during your co-op or internship.

Your Boss, your Peers and Managing How You Are Perceived at Work

Your boss or supervisor is the most influential person determining your success during an internship or co-op. Winning with him/her is a must if you are searching for a full-time offer. Even if you are uncertain about working full time at this company, there are important long-term benefits of practicing to win with your boss at this early stage.

The most important first step at a co-op or internship (or full-time role) is to establish trust with your boss. Students who do that have:

• Set up a good working relationship where they are aligned on what is expected

• Established a good frequency (cadence) of updating them to keep them informed

• Established the habit of giving/receiving feedback with them and act to make improvements based on feedback

This is all about making your boss comfortable with you. Many co-ops, interns, even full-time professionals over-look this simple but important practice of giving your boss peace of mind you are aligned on the work needed and can consistently correct actions based on feedback.

For example, in the beginning of a co-op or internship, international students usually try to prove how intelligent they are

184

by figuring out how to accomplish their tasks quickly and efficiently. While it is important to prove to your boss you are smart, spending too much effort showcasing this has too high of an opportunity cost. If you are aligned with your boss, you would have removed perception barriers that allow them to see all of your qualities (not just your smarts). You can even make up for your deficiencies in certain areas if you can demonstrate that you can acknowledge those deficiencies and work towards improving them. Developing that trust early on is an important step that should not be neglected, and it will allow your qualities to come across more clearly.

It won't always be easy to gain your boss's trust, or you might just get unlucky and get a bad boss. The above rules still apply, don't be discouraged.

The other key piece that many professionals overlook is to get others (your peers, boss's boss, etc.) to be an advocate of you. You won't be able to really understand this concept until you manage others yourself. When you are in that situation (when you're the boss) you must advocate for your team (to HR, to your boss, to other cross-functional teams, etc.), and that is much easier when others are already saying good things about your team. Getting others to advocate for you makes your boss's job even easier. They won't have to do as much work to convince others that you are a strong candidate for a full-time offer. Showcasing your qualities and ensuring that others in the organization can vouch for you will be key, particularly towards the end of your co-op or

NTERNATIONAL STUDENT HANDBOOK

internship.

Take this scenario, for example: You are in a six-month co-op, you have aligned with your boss on expectations, performed exceptional work, and are looking for a permanent position post-graduation. Once you find a role that suits you, your boss will be an advocate with the hiring team for that role and that will get you only 50% of the way to getting an offer. Another 25% will be if they believe you would be a good fit with your new team, and the rest will be your boss's boss and your current team's impression of you. Ultimately, showcasing that you can get along with others, and work well with them, becomes just as important as doing an excellent job with your tasks. If others can vouch for you based on your time as a co-op or intern, it will make your boss even more comfortable in recommending, and pushing, to get you a full-time offer. You will have established "social proof" of your qualities and will have carved out the rest of the path to secure a role.

What to Do to Make Your Work Recognized

We discussed the importance of perception vs. work quality in a previous chapter. This is imperative with your internship or co-op. Let's look at how the typical, smart and intelligent international student performs:

186

Smart//Intelligent co-op or intern:

- First day at work - seems friendly, personable and intelligent
- Completes all required reading and training in a timely fashion
- Takes instruction on their first task well, asks good questions specific to the task they must complete
- Begins task. Frequently checks in with their boss to show progress and ask questions to ensure the work is being done correctly
- Completes their task with high quality and on time
- Gets a new task and asks even better questions to ensure their work will be completed well. Follows the process above and completes the task with high quality and ahead of schedule
- Repeats above performance throughout their co-op or internship, and gets average to good feedback and ratings from their boss

Qualities Demonstrated: critical thinking, ability to complete work on time

International students have the habit of putting their head down to focus and crush their assigned tasks. They are happy to check their work frequently with their boss and showcase what they have accomplished. When done with the task at hand, they await the next task, and expect their time at the co-op or internship to be spent completing one task after another. They assume their boss is impressed that they have completed their work quickly and with quality because the results are tangible.

It's highly likely that their boss would not have had the time to check their work thoroughly at any moment during the co-op or internship. They can see the work was done on time and spot check it was done correctly. And that is the expected level performance for a co-op or intern. Anything less would make you a liability vs. an asset. It's also unlikely that the boss told anyone about the student's accomplishments or usually even kept track of the work they had been doing. The boss now has to prepare another task for the student and likely sit down to explain how to use the tools needed to accomplish that task.

So, often, completing a task becomes a moment when the boss has to invest more time out of their busy schedule to detail the next work item, making it a challenge for them. That same moment for the student is one of accomplishment (they did a good job and got the work done on or ahead of time)! These two feelings are at odds, and repeat themselves throughout all co-ops and internships. This presents an opportunity for you to win even more with your boss and to showcase your work more broadly to the rest of the team.

What can you do to ensure a better experience for your boss and a better outcome for your task accomplishment?

Let's take a look at this example of a student who understands the importance of perception and practices it:

Smart//Intelligent co-op or intern <u>aware of value of perception and prioritizes it</u>:

• First day at work - seems friendly, personable and intelligent

• Completes all required reading and training in a timely fashion

• Takes instruction on their first task well, asks good questions specific to the task they must complete. Asks about the purpose of the task. What is the higher-level goal and how will it improve the business?

• Sets up time with peers to explain what they have been tasked with, and what the high-level purpose is. Picks their brain on best ways to execute the task and gets ideas on what future related tasks might be (to achieve the higher-level objective)

• Completes their task and shows their work to peers they have built a rapport with (those who gave them time and feedback in the past). Asks them for feedback on the task and for advice on what task to propose next to their boss. Asks what tools are needed for the next task and how they can learn them (or who can teach them).

• Shows boss completed task, lets them know that peers helped

• Suggests 1 or 2 ideas for the next task, and that they identified the tools they need and how they can learn to use them

• Repeats above throughout their co-op, gets good to excellent feedback and ratings from their boss

Qualities Demonstrated: critical thinking, ability to complete work on time, ability to make decisions, dependability, communication and persuasion, team building, proactiveness, scrappiness and resourcefulness

This is how the best co-ops or interns I've interacted with perform. The black text is what they do that is incremental to the first student's example. Here is how you can repeat their success in your co-op or internship:

After getting your first instruction on your task from your boss, ask what the purpose of the task is. What question is it answering? What problem is it solving? Let your boss tell you. Next, take this opportunity to set up a meeting with another peer from your team. Explain to them what you are working on, what the purpose is, and ask their opinion and if you can pick their brain. Come prepared with questions and jot down key insights that help you understand the problem better. You can repeat this with another peer, getting more insights.

Once you are closer to completing your task, ask them if you can pick their brain again, this time for ideas on what a logical next step would be to get closer to accomplishing the overarching purpose of the task. Ask them what tools you would need and if they would help with showing you how to use them, or if they know someone else that can help.

Once you complete your task, let your boss know those peers supported you with understanding the bigger picture, that you have a suggestion for the next step, and that you have lined up someone to help walk you through the tool you need to accomplish that task. Your boss will be impressed. You would have showcased several qualities: team building, team fit, proactiveness, scrappiness/resourcefulness, and critical thinking. Even if your boss had a different task in mind, you can say yes quickly to that new task, showcasing your flexibility. Your perceived value will undoubtedly increase. Your boss and your peers now know what you are working on and know you a little better.

If at this time, you can't understand the value in doing the work above, I recommend trying it anyway. Building connections with others, being proactive, and showcasing your work to more people is incredibly valuable to you and your career. Also, getting other more experienced peers' perspectives on the problem you are trying to solve will increase the quality of your work, so you will improve both measures. The point here is to remember that how you are perceived is the most important aspect of your success with that company and that practicing how to manage how you are perceived is always a worthwhile effort.

I want to add a final point on relationships, whether with your peers or your boss. You won't necessarily get along with everyone. But similarly, to your efforts to make friends or network, in time you will find those who you get along with at work, and those who advocate for you. What's important through this process is to have some standards for yourself. Personally, I have affirmations (work commandments) that I stick closely to, regarding my relationships with others. I'm sharing them below as they have been useful to me. Use them if they resonate with you or create some of your own.

My Work Commandments:

1. Status will not determine how I treat others

I try to ignore status as much as possible. So, if someone is an entry level employee or a VP, I generally will treat them the same. If I pay too much attention to status, like I've seen others do, I'll either give away my power right from the beginning of an interaction or I will assume too much of it. I want to be my authentic self as often as possible. This allows me to be confident, regardless of who I am talking to. Some people turn into putty when they talk to higher level leaders. I work to make sure my voice tone is the same, and that my thinking and logic is not altered. I try to keep my power for myself (not drop it at the sight of someone who I think has status in the company).

2. Mutual respect guides me, always

I let mutual respect guide me in determining who I want to build a closer relationship with. Everyone I interact with gets a fair chance initially. But over time, if their response is delayed or curt more often than not, or if I sense they are not fully present in our conversations, or sense generally that they lack interest in building a relationship with me, I'll let them go. I'll do this after 2 to 3 interactions. This standard sometimes doesn't help me, as there are people who I need to win over (boss's boss, etc.) even if I don't click with them. So, my tactic is to find people who I do jive with, and who can be my advocates in front of the folks I don't click with.

3. I will leverage the Power of Reciprocity often

I believe in give and take. If I need something, some sort of help or assistance with a project, an email, a meeting, whatever, I'm not afraid to ask for it. I'm also very giving. I not only respond to people's requests for help, I react quickly to help them. Often, I offer it before they ask. With this give and take strategy, I get a lot of leverage in the company because of the network I end up building. To figure out what you can ask for, and from whom, experimentation is key. To do it, always offer someone something first. The principle of reciprocity suggests they will naturally want to give you something back. It works, trust me.

4. Avocados and Coconuts are still people

I keep the avocado vs. coconut concept in mind with all interactions. What the heck is that you may ask? It's a way to tell how to manage relationships with people, from meeting them the first time. Some people are hard on the outside, and it takes more than a few interactions to win them over, but once you do, you really start to get to know them and usually are pleasantly surprised by how nice they are. Those are the coconuts. Hard on the outside, soft on the inside.

The other type is super friendly at the surface. Sometimes, they may seem overly friendly. They are easy to get along with and usually have good networks within the company. It's also often true that they guard their secrets, their personal agenda, and often their personal lives very closely. There's a limit to how closely you can get to know them. Those are the avocados. Soft on the outside, hard seed on the inside. More than anything, this concept helps set my expectations when I'm meeting someone new.

These are my affirmations. Feel free to borrow them, and if you have some other ones that you go by, I'd love to hear about them.

Thrive on Feedback

During your co-op or internship, source feedback frequently, from as many people as possible. Although the feedback can be hard to swallow if it points out areas that you could improve, be open to it. Even if you don't agree with it, listen and focus on what led that person to give that feedback, and then act on it.

Acknowledge that you still have a lot to learn as you go into a new work environment. If you come in leaning too heavily on your strengths, you risk having blind spots with where you are falling short with your performance. Getting feedback frequently, internalizing what it means, and acting on it, is how you will improve in a shorter amount of time than the average student.

Feedback is a learning opportunity in disguise. Normally, we seek standard learning opportunities when we want to learn new skills. Examples: going back to school, attending seminars/webinars, reading books, etc. Getting feedback is an underrated and very often unused tactic that can dramatically improve your skill set once you learn how to take advantage of it. It's also free. If you have a learning mindset, then detailed feedback from your peers/boss/family can give you personalized and specific next steps to focus on.

There are 5 things you need to work on to insert this activity into your life:

1. Build the habit of asking for (and giving) feedback

2. Recognize that the way you ask (and give) feedback should be different based on seniority/closeness of the person to you

3. Push to get specific and actionable feedback (not a wishy-washy "that was good or bad" reaction)

4. Practice incorporating (ASAP) that feedback into all your upcoming work and personal interactions

5. This one is a bonus, only for Ballers . . . show or tell the person who gave you the feedback how you used it in a situation and what the result was (and thank them again)

More details below:

1. Opportunities for asking for feedback: on an email, a presentation, or a meeting. If you are working on improving your writing, you can ask your boss or peers to review an email for you

(is it concise? does it clearly state the purpose of the email? Is the grammar/vocab ok?)

2. You can ask anyone for feedback: boss, peer, family. Asking your mom for feedback differs from asking your boss (remember your boss is evaluating your performance - a good boss should give you feedback regularly). You have to be a bit more formal when asking your boss for feedback, while asking a peer can be more casual. Example - peer: "hey, any thoughts on how the meeting went?" vs. boss: "I think the meeting went well, not sure if Tom really paid attention, wonder if I could have done something differently to get my point across."

3. Get specific and actionable feedback: "Your presentation was ok" vs. "I liked your voice projection (was clear across the room), but I feel the content could have been more concise when you discussed results/next steps, etc." Push for the latter. For folks not used to giving this kind of feedback you will need to insist they give you something usable. Ask them for feedback by saying "what could have gone better" and insist they give you at least one thing. Thank the person for this great gift they have given you.

- Example of the worst feedback ever: "You are doing great! Don't change a thing". If you hear this often, then you are not learning or growing. If you hear this once in a blue moon, celebrate it and move on quickly.

4. Apply the feedback soon after you get it: on the very next email/presentation/meeting. Once you incorporate the feedback, you will start making it a habit. The fresher it is in your head, the better.

Remember, all of the above is only possible if you have (and continue to develop) a "learning" mindset. If you truly have that mindset, you will view specific and actionable feedback as one of the best gifts you can receive from someone. This is counter-intuitive, as most people have negative feelings about feedback. They feel it means they are not performing well, and therefore it affects their self-confidence. People with a "fixed" mindset take feedback as a cue they are not doing a good job vs. as an opportunity to self-reflect and learn.

That was me for a long time in my personal life and throughout my career. Now that you are aware of this personal mental block when it comes to feedback, you can take teeny tiny steps to overcome it. Slowly but surely, you will see yourself change. Take advantage of this wonderful, free resource available to you.

On Meetings and dealing with "free" time at work

Every meeting you attend during a co-op or internship is an opportunity to increase your perceived value. We've talked a lot about how important it is to manage how you are perceived, and how to keep this point top of mind when working with people (peers, boss, etc.). Meetings, especially the ones you are invited to (vs. the ones you organize), are handed to you as an opportunity to take advantage of (to improve how you are perceived).

Unfortunately, most international students don't view them as opportunities. Most even don't look forward to them and pray they don't have to say anything at them. I've seen it too often and I've also been that person many times.

Personally, meetings give me anxiety. Part of why I feel that way is likely the lack of public speaking exposure in high school and undergrad, and part is just how I'm wired. The bottom line is that my decision to avoid speaking in meetings is related to fear and anxiety. I've since overcome this fear, by working on myself internally and more importantly, exposing myself to speaking in meetings at every opportunity. Practicing in real life is so important, I can't stress that enough. Especially in your co-op or internship, where your peers and boss understand that you are learning, so your performance in this area is not heavily judged. Take advantage! Look to each meeting as an opportunity to practice. Even if you get one sentence in, it's better than nothing.

I always tell my students -

"If you were physically at a meeting, but you didn't say anything, were you really there?"

"What value did you contribute to the meeting? . . . If you didn't attend the meeting, would the outcome of the meeting have changed?"

"Even if you were invited just to get exposure (to what's being talked about and to other people), will you really internalize what you heard, and will people remember you if you didn't say anything?".

Make it count.

Here's what to do.

Meeting Basics

Though these may seem basic, they are very important, so make a mental note to follow them.

1. Show up on time. Know when each of your meetings will take place in the day and how to get there in advance, so you arrive on time.

2. Bring a notepad and pen. Don't go to a meeting empty-handed. Take notes even if it's just for notetaking sake. It will make you appear like you are engaged and interested. It'll be great also to jot down any questions you might think of, that might not make sense to ask at the meeting directly but make sense to follow up with later.

3. Don't slouch or sit inappropriately. You need to at least appear like you are paying attention (even if you can't concentrate in that moment for whatever reason).

Speaking up in Meetings

You are not expected to know everything you need to know when you start an internship or co-op. People understand that you are there to learn . . . So, learn.

When you don't know something, ask a question. When you have an idea related to the discussion, say it, so you can hear others' opinions or feedback. Do this at every meeting. If you are experiencing fear or anxiety in meetings (like I have), prepare in advance. You should know what the discussion topics are in advance, can come up with at least one question before the meeting, and then find the right time to ask it during the meeting. Preparing won't take away the fear, it will make your action (while being afraid) more manageable (easier to do).

Other than asking questions or expressing an opinion, you can ask your boss (in advance of the meeting) if it would be ok to share what you are working on with the group. You can share steps you've taken on your project or insights you have found. With this, you will have to prepare more in advance, but honestly, there isn't a better activity you could be working on during your co-op or internship in the U.S. Presenting and speaking in meetings about your tasks is exactly what you need to be practicing and exposing yourself to.

One final idea is if the meeting discussion leads to talking about next steps, you can volunteer for one of them. Just volunteering is a great way for you to make an excuse to work with new people, and for people to pay attention to who you are and what you bring to the table.

Don't let a meeting pass by without you having participated in some way . . . even if all you do is ask a relevant question.

Stepping up your Meeting game

Particularly when meeting your boss, you want to arrive ready every time. Example: let's say you were meeting your boss to discuss data you recently pulled. You could present that data on a computer screen or on printed paper. Make sure that the meeting starts with that content readily available. I can't tell you how often my co-ops spend 5 or 10 mins at the beginning of a meeting just pulling up the document they were planning to share. Please avoid that.

You will also likely have regular check-in meetings with your boss, and ideally, you are well prepared for those. A well-prepared meeting includes forwarding an agenda to your boss in advance, managing the time in your meeting to cover the most important topics (don't let all the time pass on just one topic if you have multiple to cover), and sending them a follow-up note on what the next steps are. This may seem excessive but will likely be very well received. If your boss thinks it's unnecessary, they will tell you. All's good, nothing lost. Following this format with any meeting that you organized will be well received by your peers as well. It inspires confidence that you are on top of your work and invites people to comment on your work to others (which helps with how you are perceived).

With meetings you don't organize, a good way to step in is to volunteer to take notes on what was discussed. This entails capturing the discussion notes, then summarizing the key points to share after the meeting. It's a great way to keep practicing your language and writing skills, to stay alert and focused in meetings, and it shows you take initiative.

Does everything I suggest sound like a ton of work? Yes. It does.

This advice is for those who are ready to stand out and want ideas on what works. If you are like me (a bit lazy) I suggest trying all of these ideas at least one time, to experiment and gauge others' reactions. If you find something you like and feel helps boost how you are perceived, great! You can keep doing that one thing.

Dealing with "free" time at work

With internships or co-ops that last longer periods of time, it's not uncommon for there to be "lulls" or boring periods in students' experiences. Especially towards the end of the program. By then they are likely ramped up on what they need to know to execute their job, they are more familiar with the people, and they might feel like they are just plugging away, not necessarily learning at the fast pace they once were. Lots of students welcome this "lull" as an opportunity to relax before starting classes again.

Honestly, if you need the mental break, by all means take it. If you can find more energy in the tank, you could use this time to practice your networking skills. Co-ops and internships are the BEST learning opportunities you can get while attending university in the U.S., try to make your time with them count:

• Practice telling new people what you are working on, how it relates to the big picture (what high-level problem you are working on solving?). Tell anyone that will listen, it's your pitch of how you add value to the company.

• Try to have lunch with a different person or different group every day.

• Anytime you are stuck looking for something to talk about, ask questions. Questions should relate to your work (these are an easier way to start a conversation, as working in the same company is a super legitimate similarity you have with your peers).

• If you are interested in a different type of role or department than your current one, discuss that with your boss to find some contacts in new areas and ask for informational coffee chats (you can get a ton of great insight in a short amount of time).

Always keep your Next Career Move in mind

Regardless of what your career goals are, whether you have defined them or not, you want to think about the next steps sooner than later. Time will pass quickly in an internship or co-op, and you want to avoid thinking about what you could've or should've done towards the end of your program. Think about that stuff at the beginning.

To recap, from the beginning of your co-op/internship, ask yourself what the high-level problem you or your boss or your team is working on and continue to ask questions until you have a strong understanding of how your task(s) tie to this high-level problem. I'm being repetitive on purpose. I want you to be leaders in your roles, not just clogs in the machine. Understanding why a company does what it does, who its customers are and how they keep things running is important to your career progression regardless of wanting leadership roles in the future or not. Your internship/co-op is an opportunity to learn something books can't teach you. It's an inside look into how companies function.

Set goals prior to starting your co-op or internship

If you are like I was when I was an undergrad (clueless and not sure what I wanted from a co-op or internship), then you have to step back and set goals for yourself. Thinking through "what do I want to get out of this" program will help you uncover insights about yourself and what you want to do in the future as well.

Try to write down very specific personal goals.

Here are some examples:
• Do you want to work there full time?
• Do you want to learn a new skill?
• Do you want to explore different roles?

- Do you want to be more comfortable in corporate environments?

• Do you want to learn how to better integrate with Americans?

• Do you want more opportunities to practice speaking in meetings or to groups?

No goal is too big or too small. Write down something specific, keep editing it if needed, and remind yourself daily of that goal. This exercise will help translate your actions during the co-op/internship to align with what you want out of it.

Work on your resume mid-way through the program

Add your work experience to your resume sooner than later. A common mistake students make is to wait until the end of their program to write the bullets (because then, they have completed their time there and can capture the bullets more accurately). That's nice, but not the goal. The goal is to write resume bullets that are appealing to potential employers that are similar to the company you are in now. How would you know what sounds appealing? Start writing these bullets early, preferably midway through your program, when you'll have enough context of what you've done there to get some good content, and then check them with more senior people in your team (including your boss). Use feedback to continue iterating on content throughout the rest of your time in the program, so that by the end, you have a solid and attractive set of bullets (that you know would resonate with similar employers). Feedback from your peers and manager is key here. Don't wait until you've left to get it.

8. Final Thoughts

"I've missed more than 9000 shots in my career.

I've lost almost 300 games.

26 times, I've been trusted to take the game winning shot and missed.

I've failed over and over and over again in my life.

And that is why I succeed."

~ Michael Jordan ~

So . . . what should you do now?

There's a reason you've picked up this book. There is a reason you've read this far. Some of you are in the mode of desperately trying to get a job. Others are being challenged by their journey in the U.S. and are looking for some guidance. Some have started their first co-op, or are trying to get a glimpse of what's to come with the next steps in their career. Whatever your reason, big or small, I hope I helped a bit.

I hope this book can continue to be a source of reference for you. Most importantly, take whatever resonated with you and apply it ASAP. You need to figure out how to make the advice work for you. Start very small, and keep progressing from there. Remember that you are learning, you are growing, failures and missteps are normal, and that it will all be worth it if you keep trying. Remember to be kind to yourself along the way.

Now, if you are overwhelmed by all this and are still not sure where to start, or how to think about what you want to get out of life or your career . . . I'm going to suggest you play a little game.

It's a training game that will force you to push yourself, develop good habits, improve your skills, and 10X your chances of finding an opportunity (job) that's right for you (and one you want). This game is the best possible form of exercise to improve your chances of finding a job during your U.S. academic journey. Period. Better than any academic class you have taken, better than any career fair, talk or networking event you attended. This is a bold claim. I don't make it lightly. Here are the details.

The game is called **"Challenge 28"**. You can start this game at any time in your journey, whether you just landed in the U.S. or are graduating in 3 weeks and need to find a job ASAP.

Your Objective: Reach out to 10 strangers per week for informational interviews. Optimally, these would be people who currently work full time at companies you would consider working for. Talk to two per week, 20-30 min conversations each. Do this for 14 weeks straight.

Between the research to find contacts (~2hrs), sending out 10 notes asking for time to meet (~30mins), chatting to two people (~1hr), this is no more than a 4-hour commitment per week.

Being a university student is a once in a lifetime legitimate excuse to reach out to anyone for any information (that supports your academic or career pursuit). Use the tips in this book to come up with a plan and an approach. Reach out via LinkedIn, connect with someone from a career fair or a professional who gave a talk at your school. It doesn't matter where or how you met them. Get your two, one on one conversations, done per week.

Make sure that your learnings from these calls accumulate meaningfully for you. For example, you could target only people who work at Amazon (there are over half a million Amazon employees worldwide, you shouldn't have a problem finding 10 to reach out to per week). These interviews will allow you to go deep and learn a lot more about the company. Alternatively, you can target individuals from multiple companies, with a focus on supply chain or analytics, etc. If you are curious about the kind of roles that exist in different industries, you could spend this time looking for people to learn more about "a day in the life" of those roles.

If all of this is too much, or you are not sure where to start, my advice is to JUST START. Reach out to whoever. Just go through the exercise to help make this activity normal and secondhand nature for you. As you get started, make sure you pay attention to what works with your style, what doesn't and keep experimenting to find your true voice. If you click with someone, maybe you can ask them for feedback on how you did. When you get good at these conversations, they will feel truly dynamic, where you can easily guide the discussion based on what the other person is saying, to learn more about them and their company. Don't just go through the motions in these conversations, try to home in on what works for you for keeping up good conversations.

If you succeed, I want you to share what you learned with me on social media (*#challenge28*) and how it helped. I'm rooting for you. Good luck!

My Story

Where I'm from, and why I can relate to the international student's journey to the U.S. is a bit complicated. My father is Palestinian, my mom is Lebanese, I was born in Michigan, but grew up in Al Ain, U.A.E. (family moved there soon after I was born).

I've always struggled to answer the question, "Where are you from?". The answer is not straightforward, so I say something different every time, depending on the context. Culturally, I am Middle Eastern. When I moved to the U.S. for undergrad, I experienced culture shock just like the rest of my friends who left the U.A.E. What's not similar to your experience is that I didn't face the visa struggles. And admittedly, that's why I don't talk a lot about visas in this book. I've read up a lot, talked to a bunch of students regarding their struggles related to visas, and realize ultimately that it's an evolving situation depending on the current U.S. administration's policy. Plus, there are a ton of good resources out there. I chose not to write much about it because it's not my truth, and more importantly, I believe that over-thinking the visa situation distracts students from focusing on skills they need to develop to succeed with finding a job.

Again, while I didn't struggle with the visa situation, I wasn't exactly welcomed as an American. I don't belong anywhere, and I belong everywhere at the same time. I am a Global Citizen (also known as a "Third culture kid"). I'll explain.

The U.A.E. has one of the most diverse populations in the world. Around 80%+ are expats, from Asian, Middle Eastern, European and other countries. Expats (which I was) have to pay for private school (there's no public-school option), which is typically made up of very culturally diverse cohorts. Lots of these schools had names that started with "International school of ...".

Growing up, I went to churches, mosques, and temples with friends. Every one of their homes had a new foreign culture, and set of rules and traits. It forced me to identify as Middle Eastern, to understand where I fit in, but by the time I left the U.A.E., I'll tell you I could hardly relate to Middle Easterners. My parents were from different countries, so I struggled to form a specific identity early on (e.g., the way you say "Egg" in Palestine differs from how you say it in Lebanon, and the household was divided on such topics). Generally, I was also picked on because my Arabic was very choppy.

When I moved to the U.S., it was obviously hard to relate to Americans, but I also struggled to relate to Middle Easterners. I later felt this was a positive outcome because it forced me to engage with anyone and everyone. I had my own diverse set of friends (like five, not more, I was super introverted then). I also learned then that not everyone that is from one country and grew up in the same town or city their whole life, necessarily felt like they "fit in" growing up.

There are many students who have yearned for some time during high school and before, to leave and see and experience something different. They weren't just searching for familiar things or people, and when I crossed paths with them, we naturally clicked.

Later in my professional life, my roles at U.S. companies all involved international operations in one form or another. Through work, I travelled across the U.S., Europe, and the Middle East. I travelled to different parts of Mexico, to China and Singapore. Those experiences are my most cherished from my career. I met my wife at work, who was from a different culture, country, and religion. At that point in my life, I already could not focus on differences between cultures unless I thought about them. She also yearned to explore outside her home country from as early as her high school years. We were a natural fit.

A few years later, when I did my MBA (thanks to my wife pushing me), I searched for a school where I could immerse myself in new, international experiences. We moved to Singapore for a year where we traveled across most of Southeast Asia with our 1-year old son. It was one of the best experiences in my life.

Today, I'm in my thirties, and I don't feel like I'm from anywhere. In the Middle East, I'm treated like an American. In the U.S., it's clear that I'm not American (I still can't get myself to like American Football or Baseball -- hot dogs and wings yes!). There isn't a single place I can just fit in nicely. For a while, this thought was a self-ailment.

Today, I use this identity to stand out. I am the international guy at work. I'm bold about it and express my thoughts, accent, and controversial ideas without hesitation. When you are Muslim, Middle Eastern and your wife is a Catholic Mexican . . . what do you have to lose in the Trump era of the U.S.? Seriously, I just don't care anymore about how people judge me. You can make these facts work for you or against you. It's ultimately up to you. I will continue to be myself. Granted, it took some awkward moments to figure out how much of my thoughts and opinions are ok to share, but I'm getting better at it day by day.

In the Middle East, I'm the American guy. They literally call me that, even though I speak Arabic and like Molokhia (for those who have no idea what I'm talking about, it's a spinach type, slimy leaf stewed and eaten in different ways in the Middle East). I like the whole leaf kind, not the minced kind, yuck! Apologies to my Egyptian friends.

In Mexico, there are a lot of Lebanese Mexicans, who immigrated to Mexico many years ago. So, people have some familiarity with Lebanese culture, and therefore I tell them I am Lebanese. It helps. I also love tacos el pastor with pineapple, onions, and cilantro and I put salsa verde on everything . . . I'm practically Mexican at this point. I feel good about all this, and I wish it didn't take me so long to appreciate and enjoy this as my truth.

If I had a mentor when I was starting my career, the one thing I really needed to hear would have been "don't worry". Just don't. You are who you are, and if you haven't found your true voice yet (like I hadn't for a while), you will. Just keep plugging away. Know there are many people rooting for you to succeed; your family, friends, and some kind souls you meet along the way. Good luck!

Quotes to help you along the way

On Purpose . . .

"Finding yourself is not really how it works. You aren't a ten dollar bill in last winter's coat pocket. You are also not lost. Your true self is right there, buried under cultural conditioning, other people's opinions, and inaccurate conclusions you drew as a child and adult that became your beliefs about who you are. Finding yourself is actually returning to yourself. An unlearning, an excavation, a remembering who you were before the world got its hand on you."

~ Emily McDowell ~

"We have all a better guide in ourselves, if we would attend to it, than any other person can be."

~ Jane Austen ~

"Life isn't about finding yourself. Life is about creating yourself."

~ George Bernard Shaw ~

"Control your own destiny or someone else will."

~ Jack Welch ~

"Remember that wherever your heart is, there you will find your treasure."

~ Paulo Coelho, The Alchemist ~

"The value of our lives is not determined by what we do for ourselves. The value of our lives is determined by what we do for others."

~ Simon Sinek ~

"One of the huge mistakes people make is that they try to force an interest on themselves. You don't choose your passions; your passions choose you."

~ Jeff Bezos ~

"Everything is energy and that's all there is to it. Match the frequency of the reality you want and you cannot help but get that reality. It can be no other way. This is not philosophy. This is physics."

~ Albert Einstein ~

"The two most important days in your life are the day you are born and the day you find out why."

~ Mark Twain ~

On Determination . . .

"Keep exploring. Keep dreaming. Keep asking why. Don't settle for what you already know. Never stop believing in the power of your ideas, your imagination, your hard work to change the world."

~ Barack Obama ~

"Today I will do what others won't, so tomorrow I can do what others can't"

~ Jerry Rice ~

"If opportunity doesn't knock, build a door."

~ Milton Berle ~

"If it is important to you, you will find a way. If not, you will find an excuse."

~ unknown ~

On Faith . . .

"Believe you can and you're halfway there."

~ Theodore Roosevelt ~

"You have power over your mind - not outside events. Realize this, and you will find strength."

~ Marcus Aurelius ~

"Don't limit yourself. Many people limit themselves to what they think they can do. You can go as far as your mind lets you. What you believe, remember, you can achieve."

~ Mary Kay Ash ~

"If a heart is filled with faith, it will guide you to the truth."

~ Ibn Arabi ~

"Faith is having a positive attitude about what you can do and not worrying at all about what you can't do."

~ Joyce Meyer ~

On Change . . .

"Often, people who can do, don't because they're afraid of what people that can't do will say about them doing."

~ Trevor Noah ~

"We spend so much time being afraid of failure, afraid of rejection. But regret is the thing we should fear the most."

~ Trevor Noah ~

"A shark in a fish tank will grow 8 inches, but in the ocean it will grow to 8 feet or more. The shark will never outgrow its environment and the same is true about you. Many times we're around small thinking people so we don't grow. Change your environment and watch your growth."

~ unknown ~

"The most important spiritual growth doesn't happen when you're meditating or on a yoga mat. It happens in the midst of conflict -- when you're frustrated, angry or scared and you're doing the same old thing, and then you realize that you have a choice to do it differently . . ."

~ unknown ~

"What we achieve inwardly will change outer reality."

~ Plutarch ~

"Change has a considerable psychological impact on the human mind. To the fearful, it is threatening because it means that things may get worse. To the hopeful, it is inspiring because the challenge now exists to make things better."

~ Whitney Young Jr. ~

"It's never too late or, in my case, too early to be whoever you want to be. You can change or stay the same; there are no rules to this thing. And I hope you see things that startle you. I hope you see things you never felt before. I hope you meet people with a different point of view. I hope you live a life you're proud of. If you find that you're not, I hope you have the strength to start all over again."

~ F. Scott Fitzgerald ~

"If you NEVER did, you SHOULD. These things are FUN, and FUN is good!"

~ Dr. Seuss ~

"A mind that is stretched by new experience will never go back to its old dimensions."

~ Oliver Wendell Holmes, Jr. ~

On Mentors . . .

"A mentor is someone who allows you to see the hope inside yourself."

~ Oprah Winfrey ~

"Sometimes you can't see yourself clearly until you see yourself through the eyes of others."

~ Ellen DeGeneres ~